This Wounded Land

This Wounded Land

THE ERA OF RECONSTRUCTION
1865-1877

by IRVING WERSTEIN

DELACORTE PRESS / NEW YORK, N.Y.

This book is for
CANDIDA,
who opened many doors

Author's Note

FOR OVER A CENTURY, the Reconstruction Period has been depicted as an era of tyranny and repression in the conquered South. The stereotype of the conniving, ruthless Carpetbagger come to plunder the defeated Southerners and to defraud the simple, confused former slaves is a familiar one in American history.

Only the proudly defiant ex-Confederate has emerged unsullied from the cruel Reconstruction years. This Southern knight, overflowing with chivalry and devotion to a Lost Cause, apparently had only two purposes in life: the first, to shield Southern womanhood from leering Carpetbaggers and lecherous ex-slaves; the second, to keep untarnished the glorious traditions of the Old South. To do this he resorted to dubious methods. He taught the Carpetbaggers "a lesson" with whip and gun; he kept the "blacks" in line with whip, gun and lynch rope.

It was the "Unreconstructed Rebel" who donned the robes of the Ku Klux Klan, spreading terror in the night with fiery crosses and arsonist's torches. Somehow, the

Klansman, and what he stood for, survived in our history more as a folk hero than an assassin and bully.

The entire Reconstruction Period has been, until recently, interpreted in a distorted fashion; some scholars studied the era through the wrong end of the telescope. Seldom were the achievements of the time mentioned; only the bad and inglorious deeds were repeated.

I have attempted, in this book, to give my young readers a different point of view of the Reconstruction years. I do not claim that this is a definitive work on the subject; it is merely an illumination of a controversial time in American history.

I have chosen to cast my beam on those phases of Reconstruction days only infrequently exposed to light. I believe I have treated without prejudice those crucial years when the opportunity to create a New South based on democracy and civil justice was badly fumbled by men who lacked the foresight and courage to carry through a basic American concept.

Although an author works alone, he is often helped along the way. I have had the good fortune to be assisted by many kind people who made my path much easier. Among them were Leon Weidman, American History Room, New York Public Library; Dr. James J. Heslin, Director, New-York Historical Society, and the excellent library staff of the Society; Dr. Philip Van Doren Stern, the well-known historian; Mr. Sidney B. Solomon and Mr. Henry Chafetz of the Pageant Book Store, who provided out-of-print source books; my agent, Miss Candida Donadio; Mrs. Lee Levin, who typed the manuscript; my wife and my young son. There are others—Mr. Ken Johnston, of the *World Almanac* staff; Mr. Thomas J. Fanning, Information Materials Press; and the librarians at the New York Newspaper Library—all of whom I now thank wholeheartedly.

I.W.

New York, March 1967

This Wounded Land

MONDAY, MARCH 4, 1865, dawned dismally. A chill drizzle fell upon Washington, D.C., to the dismay of the thousands jamming the capital for President Abraham Lincoln's second inauguration. The weather worsened during the morning, and by noon, when the inaugural parade was to get underway, a steady rain was coming down.

According to contemporary observers, not even the foul weather could squelch the enthusiasm of the people massed four and five deep along Pennsylvania Avenue. Few seemed to mind either the rain or the thick, pasty mud that coated the sidewalks to shoetop level.

Women and girls in bright dresses, huddled under dripping umbrellas, craned to see the paraders. Men with water pouring from hat brims stood awaiting the marchers. There was cheering, laughter, happy voices. Young soldiers, self-conscious in ill-fitting uniforms, eyed the girls. On every side one saw smiling faces and heard animated talk. Abe Lincoln was being sworn in for the second time and folks had come to have fun.

It would take more than rain to spoil this day!

Precisely at noon, the inaugural parade started. Regimental colors flapped wetly in the wind; mud squished beneath the feet of the marchers as they sloshed up the unpaved avenue made swampy by the rain. Artillery caissons, hauled by straining horses, splashed mud everywhere, splattering outriders and spectators. Drums pounded a soggy cadence, trumpets gurgled, and fifes gargled, as bandsmen sloshed through mire.

Despite the sloppy footing, marchers stepped in good array, ranks dressed, rifles aslant, guidon bearers ramrod straight. The battle-hardened soldiers marched with pride. The proudest of them was a battalion of Negro infantry; each black man held his head high, dark face sternly set, aware of this historic moment. Never before had Negro troops marched in a presidential inaugural parade.

The Negroes attracted much attention amidst all the bands, spectacular floats, fire brigades, cavalry and civic groups. Some onlookers applauded. Others glowered at the dusky-skinned riflemen. Although almost four years of war had passed, many Northerners still failed to comprehend that the struggle had been not just to restore "the Union as it was" in 1860, when the Confederate States had seceded.

Even before North and South resorted to arms, the nearly 4,000,000 Negroes held in bondage by Southern planters had been a paramount issue in the sectional controversy. When the shooting had started in April 1861, few Northerners cared one way or the other about slavery. Although the "peculiar institution" was regarded with some repugnance in the North, most Yankees never would have fought merely to win freedom for enslaved Negroes.

Only the dedicated crusaders against human bondage —the abolitionists—saw slavery as a sufficient cause for war. But the enslaved men, women and children of the South cast a long shadow over the land. If slavery had not actually triggered the war, it was an underlying factor.

The Southerners needed slaves to plow the fields, harvest the crops and work the plantations. Of course, the majority of farmers in the South were not wealthy plantation owners but proprietors of small farms from which they eked a living.

The hardworking Southern farmer, known as a "mudsill," had his counterpart in the North, where thousands of independent men toiled long and hard on the land. In North and South, the rich lived high and the poor sweated for their daily bread.

In the North, however, a rapidly expanding industrialism already had begun to drain manpower from the farms. Thousands of young men and women came to the cities to work in factories. But agriculture was the mainstay of Southern economy. Although tobacco, rice and other crops were cultivated, cotton was "King," especially for the big planter. And to raise cotton, they used slaves—as many as they could get.

The South had little industry, comparatively few railroad lines and a lack of good highways. Communications

were slow—many regions still did not have telegraph
wires.

Southern cotton growers needed more and more land.
They coveted the wide reaches of the fertile Western and
Southwestern territories so well-suited for raising cotton.
The slaveowners wanted to spread the "peculiar institution" to the territories but were fiercely opposed by anti-
slavery forces. The tensions over extending slavery to the
territories grew until that controversy and other disagree-
ments between North and South—high Northern-inspired
tariffs, Northern control of the House of Representatives
because of increased population, the rising indebtedness
of Southerners to Northern suppliers, and many more
sources of friction—finally exploded into warfare. The
nation had paid an awesome price in lives and property
losses since 1861.

The conflict that had been begun to preserve the
Union developed into something more as the cruel and
bloody years passed: it became a crusade for human liberty. Union soldiers at the fighting fronts soon found that
the war was about slavery and the morality of one man's
owning another.

As Yankees advanced into the Southland, Negroes flee-
ing servitude crossed Union lines in overwhelming numbers. The problem of how to treat the swarms of bondsmen became more acute daily. Some Union commanders,
in Virginia and elsewhere, simply returned the fugitives
to their owners. After all, they reasoned, a slave was private property and property rights had to be respected,
even those of the Rebels. However, officers with aboli-

tionist convictions refused to do this. To them slavery was the ultimate abomination and they would have no part in abetting the practice.

The U. S. Government finally decided that slaves could properly be considered as "contraband of war." A new name was coined for runaway Negroes—"contrabands." Escaped slaves proved invaluable to the Yankees. The women became cooks and laundresses; the men dug trenches, built fortifications and roads, drove wagons and ambulances. A major contribution of the "contrabands" was to serve as guides for Union troops. General William Tecumseh Sherman frankly admitted that his march from Atlanta to Savannah could not have been accomplished without the aid of fugitive slaves who pointed out trails and paths through the swamps.

After much hesitation, the War Department authorized the recruitment of Negro regiments as combat troops. By the end of the war, in April 1865, almost 200,000 slaves and Negro freedmen were under arms. They fought in many hard battles and suffered heavy casualties.

The Negro dead, maimed and wounded, the thousands of brave young black men on the firing line, gave ample evidence that the slaves did not expect freedom simply to be handed to them. They were ready and willing to fight for it. A black man needed more than ordinary courage to take his place as a Union soldier. He knew that, if captured, the Southerners would treat him as a fugitive slave, not as a prisoner of war. He would be either sold into slavery or executed on the spot.

White officers who led Negroes in battle also faced other perils; the Confederates regarded them as leaders of insurrectionists—an offence punishable by death. (The Southerners showed this was no empty threat. Fort Pillow, Tennessee, a Union stronghold, was overrun by Confederates under General Nathan Bedford Forrest, on April 12, 1864. Forrest's men massacred both the Negro garrison and their white officers after the troops had surrendered.)

Thus, with his blood and agony, the Negro became deeply involved in the war and its aftermath. He had earned a stake in the nation's future. The country could never again live as it had in the past. President Lincoln once said, "A house divided against itself cannot stand. I believe that this government cannot endure permanently half-slave and half-free."

But Lincoln remained uncertain of the course to take in dealing with the issue of slavery. "If all earthly power were given me, I should not know what to do about the existing institution," he said. Yet, despite his uncertainty, the President regarded slavery as a moral injustice that had no place in a democratic country. To him it was a blight on the nation, a barbaric anachronism. "If slavery is not wrong, nothing is wrong," he declared.

After the crucial Battle of Antietam, in September 1862, Lincoln at last made public a decision concerning the slaves. Following the acceptance of a draft read to the Cabinet in July, he issued a preliminary Emancipation Proclamation in September, to become effective on January 1, 1863. This document, which has been likened to the Magna Carta and the Declaration of Independence as a beacon of liberty, was nothing of the sort. It merely stated that, after the effective date, all slaves in those areas of the South still in rebellion were "henceforth and forever free."

Actually, not a single slave was freed. Those affected by the Emancipation Proclamation were under Confederate, not Union control. Slaves in the Border states were not set free because Lincoln feared a rebellion—there were many slaveowners in those states. As one newspaperman noted: "The principle behind this declaration is not that one human being cannot justly own another, but that he cannot own him unless he is loyal to the United States."

Despite its flaws, the Emancipation Proclamation was an important blow against slavery, although a timid one. Lincoln wanted to end slavery, but did not know how to do it.

In December 1862, addressing Congress, the President proposed that each slave state be given a chance to develop its own system of emancipation, which might be implemented over a period of years and completed by January 1, 1900. Cooperating states would receive federal financial aid in the form of interest-bearing bonds. "This slow process . . . spares both races from the evils of sudden derangement," Mr. Lincoln explained.

He also favored as a possible solution to the Negro question a plan that combined gradual emancipation and compensation to slaveowners with the resettling of freed Negroes somewhere outside the United States—perhaps

Africa, South America, Central America or the Caribbean islands. In such places, Lincoln believed, the Negroes would be more welcome than in the United States and thus spared the indignities of social and economic discrimination.

But removal of the Negroes by resettlement from the American scene seemed unworkable. Although Lincoln still felt the plan had merits, he was acutely aware that the Negro had a stake in the country earned with his sweat and blood. The President was greatly troubled because he felt the Negro would never attain equality and would always be forced by prejudice into an inferior role.

As the war dragged on and the toll mounted, Northerners realized that something drastic and fundamental had to be done for the Negro. The temper of the people indicated the desirability of such a step. Genuine disgust over slavery kept mounting. In Congress, so-called Radical Republicans—such men as Representative Thaddeus Stevens of Pennsylvania, Senator Ben Wade of Ohio, Senator Zachariah Chandler of Michigan, and Representative George W. Julian of Indiana—kept pressing for strong governmental action on slavery. Their reasons went beyond the moral issue of slavery. The Radicals feared that the Supreme Court might declare the Emancipation Proclamation to be unconstitutional. Also they were on safe ground in pressing for further action against slavery—by 1865, the crucial Border states had come firmly under Union control.

On January 1, 1865, the Thirteenth Amendment to the Constitution, which forever abolished "involuntary servitude" in the United States of America, was passed by Congress. The Union states ratified the amendment in December 1865 and the American Negro was released from bondage.

Small wonder that, in March 1865, the Negro soldiers parading on Pennsylvania Avenue should attract the eyes of so many spectators and evoke from them such mixed emotions. However, it was right and fitting for colored men in army blue to march; they had won that honor on the field of battle.Their cadenced tread along the soggy, muddy street made a martial sound; but even more than that, it symbolized the beat of a brighter future for the downtrodden and the enslaved; in those steps resounded an echo of hope.

II

THE GREAT PLAZA before the Capitol was packed with
humanity. Every inch of space seemed to be occupied
and the crowd spilled over from the square onto the
greening lawns and the shrubbery that fringed the immense concourse. Suddenly, the rain stopped and the
cloudy sky was somewhat brightened by wan sunlight.
Ringing the Capitol were ranks of infantrymen with
fixed bayonets. Off to the sides stood squadrons of cavalry and, on a hummock, an artillery battery had been
emplaced, the cannon snouts pointed at the throng. The
authorities were taking no chances with the President's
security.

Precisely at 12:45 P.M., the inaugural party appeared
upon the platfrom that had been erected on the Capitol
steps. President Lincoln was there with high-ranking
government officials, members of the Supreme Court, the
Cabinet, heads of departments, governors of states and
territories, the diplomatic corps and many other people.
Lincoln was easy to pick out. His tall, gaunt frame tow-
ered above all the rest.

As he rose to speak, a tremendous roar went up from the spectators. It echoed and reechoed like waves breaking upon a rocky coastline; the thundering shout rose ever louder until it reached a crescendo that reminded one eyewitness of "a thousand cannon firing simultaneously."

The President stood unruffled, acknowledging the ovation with a slight, sad smile. His face was lined and careworn; the strains and the burdens of the war had left their marks on the weary Chief Executive. He waited patiently for the applause to fade away. After a few minutes, the cheering died down and Lincoln prepared to speak. Before he could utter a word, a brilliant burst of sunshine flooded the city and the crowd cheered again. Some took it as an omen of good fortune. A loud voice was heard to shout, "The Lord has seen fit to smile on us! Amen!"

There was laughter and a chorus of "Amens!" and the onlookers finally settled into rapt attention. The silence was so complete that birds could be heard twittering in the trees. Without further ado, Lincoln launched his Second Inaugural Address. His rather shrill voice carried almost to the edges of the vast throng; those at the very extremities of the audience strained their ears but could not distinguish the speaker's words.

Lincoln's speech was brief. He concluded with some of the most poignant phrases ever delivered by a public figure:

> With malice toward none; with charity for all; with firmness in the right, as God gives us to see the right, let us

strive to finish the work we are in; to bind up the nation's wounds; to care for him who shall have borne the battle and for his widow, and his orphan—to do all which may achieve and cherish a just and a lasting peace among ourselves, and with all nations.

Having finished, the President bowed to the audience and the distinguished guests on the platform. There was no wild applause after he had completed the speech, no cheering, no grand demonstration. Many in the throng wept openly, remembering the boys gone off to the war; the strong, eager youths dead at Shiloh and Malvern Hill, Fair Oaks and Vicksburg, Antietam and Gettysburg, dead in a hundred lonely woods and swamps, dead on hillsides and in cornfields, their young blood staining the soil of distant places far from home.

Lincoln's words evoked memories and touched hearts. It was a masterly and beautiful speech, a gentle speech that promised reunion and brotherhood with the nearly vanquished foe.

And that was as it should be, his audience felt. There had been too much bloodshed, too much suffering, too much hatred in the land. The time for hating was done; there was need for love and understanding, not revenge. All this Lincoln had said in a few words. "With malice toward none; with charity for all."

This was the spirit and the dream.

Chief Justice Salmon P. Chase then gave the oath of office. Lincoln placed his right hand on the open pages of the Bible and swore to "preserve, protect and defend the Constitution of the United States—so help me God." He bent forward and kissed the Book. When he rose to his full six foot and four inches, Lincoln again had the authority to serve as President of the United States another four years.

As the ritual ended, the crowd cheered enthusiastically. A band played "Hail to the Chief." Cannon roared a salute. Everyone was in high spirits. Despite the inauspicious start, the day was turning out fine. Could one ask for more than brilliant sunshine, a touch of springtime and clear indications that the war would be soon over?

III

FROM THE CORDIALITY congressmen universally showed
to Lincoln at the inaugural ceremonies, nobody would
have guessed that Congress and the President were feud-
ing over the question of how to deal with the South when
the war was over. This problem had cropped up in the
earliest days of the hostilities. Although in 1861 the
South was far from defeat—indeed foreign observers
were convinced that the North would lose—neither Lincoln nor the Republican majority in Congress ever had
doubted eventual Union victory. Through the years, both
the President and congressional Republicans had known
bad times as the fortunes of battle swung back and forth;
but not even in the blackest days did they lose faith in
their ultimate victory.

On July 4, 1861, Lincoln told a special session of Congress, "Lest there be some uneasiness as to what is to be
the course of the government towards the Southern
states, after the rebellion shall have been suppressed, the
Executive deems it proper to say, it will be his purpose

then, as ever, to be guided by the Constitution and the laws."

On the surface, this statement appeared sound enough; undoubtedly, Mr. Lincoln intended to reassure the Southerners that he would not inflict harsh peace terms on them. But his statement had no meaning. He could not be guided by the Constitution or the laws. The Constitution said nothing that dealt with the existing crisis and no law covered it. There was no precedent to follow. Never before in the history of the country had such a situation occurred, nor had the Founding Fathers made any provision for this type of emergency; they had not foreseen any state's quitting the Union.

(While the Constitution does not forbid states from leaving the Union, neither does it permit them to do so. That document simply makes no mention of the subject.)

Much scholarly, long-winded constitutional opinion was voiced in Washington and Montgomery, Alabama (the first capital of the Confederacy) after the eleven Southern states had seceded.

Among the reasons they gave to justify secession on constitutional grounds, Southern leaders contended that the states were older than the Union—in 1787 they had voluntarily formed a Union, tacitly reserving for themselves the right to withdraw from it. According to Southern reasoning, the federal government existed by the will of the various states and had no power to hold them together.

On the other hand, Lincoln argued that, once in the Union, no state had a right to drop out. Each state, the

President said, had surrendered some of its sovereignty to the central government.

> Perpetuity [he declared] is implied, . . . if not expressed, in the fundamental law of all national governments. No government . . . ever had a provision in its organic law for its own termination. . . . It follows . . . that no state upon its own mere motion can lawfully get out of the Union. . . . Acts of violence, within any state or states, are insurrectionary or revolutionary according to circumstances.

If the Constitution offered no guidance about secession, neither did it describe a course for either President or Congress to take should a state or states secede. Without constitutional authority to illuminate the methods of dealing with secession, Lincoln quickly declared that a state of insurrection existed in the South. On this subject the Constitution had much to say in specific terms. In times of domestic crisis, Congress was authorized by the Constitution to "call forth the militia and suppress insurrections." Additional laws, enacted in the early days of the nation, enabled the President to use troops for the purpose of "restoring order" and "to put down combinations of disloyal citizens."

(Thus, the North was not fighting to bring seceded states back into the Union, for Lincoln never considered them to be outside of the Union. Rather he had unleashed force to crush an insurrection against the federal government. However, his position was somewhat weakened. He had blockaded Southern ports—an act of war usually taken against sovereign nations.)

Certain members of the House and Senate favored inflicting a harsh peace on the South, declaring, toward the end of the war, that the Southern states actually had seceded from the Union, founded an independent government and waged war on the United States. The North was dealing with a foreign foe, not domestic insurrectionaries, the "hard peace" men asserted. When the Confederates finally were beaten, they must be treated as vanquished enemies, not "errant brothers."

With military victory so close, Lincoln deplored this congressional attitude. In his opinion, the Union's duty after victory should be to restore the old relationship between the seceded states and the federal government. He wanted the "Union as it was."

He believed the job of accomplishing this goal belonged to the President, not Congress. As commander in chief of the army and navy, he led the nation's armed forces. Because Congress had not been in session in April 1861, Lincoln on his own authority had called out the militia and declared martial law in the South. The initial responsibility for suppressing the rebellion had fallen on the President. Lincoln, therefore, concluded that it was up to him to decide under what conditions a Southern state might reassume its place in the Union and when martial law should be revoked.

The Radical Republicans, who controlled a majority of both the House and the Senate, disagreed with the President. According to them, Congress and Congress alone, had the power to decide when the rebel states might once more be accepted into the fold, and when Southerners could enjoy representation in the House and the Senate. A jurisdictional controversy between the legislative and executive branches of government thus was touched off. Had logic prevailed, reconstruction of the Union might have been made a task shared equally by the President and Congress.

In view of the opposition in Congress, Lincoln bypassed congressional advisers and improvised a reconstruction program of his own as Union armies regained large areas of the South. In his efforts to rebuild the dismembered Union, Lincoln sought to reestablish loyal state governments in the conquered territories.

On December 8, 1863, Lincoln issued a proclamation to speed up the creation of such governments. In this proclamation, he offered an easy way for any Southern state to regain its former place and status in the Union. A minimum of ten percent of the qualified voters of 1860 was required to take an oath of allegiance to the United States. This group might then proceed to form a state government, which Lincoln would recognize. Once these steps had been completed, that state had the right to send duly elected representatives and senators to Washington.

Lincoln realized that a government supported by only ten percent of the voters was far from ideal, but it offered a rallying point around which a more substantial governmental structure could be built. According to Lincoln, the ten-percent minority government was "only as the egg to the fowl . . . but we shall sooner have the fowl by hatching the egg than by smashing it."

Lincoln's December proclamation did not sit well with

the Radicals. In the first place, they felt, he had flouted jurisdictional boundaries by undertaking duties which, in their opinion, belonged to Congress. Consequently, they took measures to wrest control of the reconstruction program from the President.

Some seven months later, in July 1864, when Congress reconvened, both houses approved a bill introduced by Senator Ben Wade of Ohio and Representative Henry W. Davis of Maryland which proposed a more severe policy for the Southern states.

Under the provisions of the Wade-Davis bill, each conquered Confederate state was to be ruled by a military governor. One of his duties was to oversee the voting enrollment and eligibility of white male citizens to hold public office. When a majority of those enrolled had taken an oath of allegiance to the United States, delegates were to be elected to a state convention which was obliged to repudiate secession and abolish slavery. Before a Southerner could qualify as a voter or a convention delegate, he had to take a second oath, known as the "iron-clad oath," in which he swore that he never voluntarily had supported the Confederacy.

This measure was passed on the last day of the session and went to Lincoln for his signature. However, he killed the bill with a "pocket veto"—which simply meant he refused to sign it. (This can be done only at the end of a session.) In taking this step, Lincoln was careful to explain that he was not "inflexibly committed to one plan of restoration." He characterized the Wade-Davis bill as a "proper plan for the loyal people of any state" and offered to let the public choose between his method and that proposed by the bill.

Ben Wade, a choleric man, railed against Lincoln for the pocket veto. "Let the President stick to his executive duties . . . and leave political reorganization to Congress," he growled. Lincoln paid no attention to the fuming Senator or to the rest of his congressional critics.

Until the time of his tragic death, Lincoln adhered to his own plan of reconstruction. When the war ended in April 1865, President Lincoln had given his approval to reconstructed governments in four states—Louisiana, Arkansas, Tennessee and Virginia—each formed according to his scheme.

Although loyal Union men had been elected as governors, Congress refused to seat senators and representatives from the former rebel states that had complied with Lincoln's terms. As one Washington resident wrote, "Old Abe and Congress have reached a stand-off. He won't give an inch nor will Congress. It's a pretty mess."

IV

FORMING LOYAL GOVERNMENTS in the onetime Confederate states was only one of the great problems posed by reconstruction. A more pressing dilemma was what should be done with the many thousands who willingly had backed the Confederate government. These people were technically liable to arrest, indictment and trial as traitors. As treason during war called for the death penalty, it was conceivable that the South would become a slaughter pen if traitors were punished in strict accordance with the law.

However, neither Lincoln nor Congress had any desire for mass executions; not even the Radicals wanted to drown the South in blood. Still, a court had no choice except to pass a death sentence on anyone found guilty of treason. Unless Congress moved rapidly, the nightmare of "firing squads and hangmen working around the clock" would become a reality.

Long before the war's conclusion was in sight, Congress had had the foresight to take a preventive measure against wholesale legal executions for treason in the South. During the summer of 1862, Congress passed a law called the Second Confiscation Act. It provided that treason might be punished by fine or imprisonment as well as the death penalty. This clause of the Act decreased the dreadful possibilities that death sentences would be passed on hundreds of Southerners after the war.

Certain other points in the Second Confiscation Act aroused considerable controversy between Lincoln and the Radicals. Congress had decreed in the Act that a person who engaged in rebellion or insurrection was to be punished by a fine, imprisonment, and the confiscation of all his property—including slaves.

Strict enforcement of this clause would have wrought a tremendous upheaval in the South, a virtual revolution. Nearly all slaves would have been seized and emancipated, large plantations broken up and redistributed, the planter aristocracy virtually wiped out economically.

Lincoln disagreed strongly with most of the Second Confiscation Act's provisions; he had no taste for revolution. Under his pressure, Congress altered the law to some extent. Land seizures were to be effective only during the lifetime of the guilty party; upon his death, all properties would be returned to the heirs.

After having gained this point, Lincoln refused to enforce the Act. As Southern territories were captured, the President took no action under the powers granted by it. No one was arrested or indicted for insurrection; no property was seized, no slave set free.

And, according to the proclamation of December 1863,

any Confederate who took an oath of allegiance to the federal government received a full pardon, which granted him immunity from the Act.

Only a handful of Southerners were not covered by this proclamation. Among them were members of the Confederate government, officers above the rank of colonel in the army, naval officers above the rank of lieutenant, men who had resigned from the U. S. Congress and federal judgeships, or given up commissions in the United States Army or Navy to join Confederate ranks. However, such persons could seek individual pardons and Lincoln indicated that he would liberally grant such requests.

How to deal with leading Confederates such as President Jefferson Davis and his cabinet members was, however, a real headache. Lincoln was not quite sure what to do with them. On more than one occasion, he privately expressed the hope that they would "skip the country" and be heard from no more. Above all, the President wished to avoid creating Southern martyrs. He was assassinated before squarely confronting the issue; but, from all indications, it appeared that he would have dealt with it in a kindly manner—even in the case of Jefferson Davis.

Only on the slavery question was Lincoln wholly indecisive. During the war's first year, he refused to interfere with the matter. Twice, Lincoln countermanded generals who had freed slaves of Confederate sympathizers in their territories. He would not enforce the emancipation clause of the Confiscation Act and, in 1862, even after

Congress had authorized the enlistment of Negroes for military duty, Lincoln hesitated for many months to enroll them. When Horace Greeley, the editor of the New York *Tribune*, made a fervent antislavery appeal to him, the President replied: "My paramount object in this struggle is to save the Union and is not either to save or to destroy slavery."

Not until September 22, 1862, with the preliminary Emancipation Proclamation, did Lincoln take action on the slavery issue. He had hoped that this step would mollify the rapidly growing abolitionist sentiment in the North. But instead of satisfying the antislavery people, Lincoln invoked their wrath. One prominent abolitionist denounced the Proclamation by describing it as "having the moral force of a bill of lading." The articulate abolitionist, Wendell Philips, criticized Lincoln for waging a "senseless war" and characterized him as a "first-rate second-rate man."

However, Lincoln was playing a politician's game. He was a strong party man and knew that, in the future, the Republican party would require the support of ex-Confederates if it were to grow in the South. His charitable attitude toward rebels was, in part, politically motivated. Abe Lincoln was, above all, a practical politician and knew that one had to do favors to win favors.

The way he handled the slavery question was ample evidence of this. Contrary to the legend that he was the "Great Emancipator," Lincoln's tactics smacked little of the crusader; he was no knight in shining armor riding forth to free the oppressed. His quest was to salvage the

Union. Even after the Emancipation Proclamation, the abolition of slavery played almost no vital part in his blueprint for reconstruction.

By 1864, it appeared that his viewpoint on slavery had shifted somewhat. The loyalty oath required an ex-Confederate to support the acts of Congress and the proclamations of the President in regard to slavery. In July, Lincoln publicly offered to give consideration to any Confederate peace proposal "embracing the restoration of the Union and the abolition of slavery." But he was not rigid about this. A month later he hinted that reunion and abolition were not irrevocably interwoven. "If Jefferson Davis wishes . . . to know what I would do if he were to offer peace and reunion, saying nothing about slavery, let him try me," Lincoln wrote.

On one point he took a firm stand. The nearly 200,000 Negroes doing military service, whether on the firing line or behind it, were never again to be enslaved, he vowed. The others—more than 3,000,000—could be made the object of negotiation. Perhaps the President still hoped that his resettlement plan might yet be put into large-scale operation. A mass exodus of Negroes from the United States surely would end that worrisome subject, he believed. But the idea never gained wide support; it was not possible to hide the issue "under the carpet." No matter how Lincoln sidestepped or equivocated, no matter how he maneuvered, the Negro continued to plague him.

After the passage of the Thirteenth Amendment, the President had to grapple with a fresh dilemma. The Negroes now had freedom, but needed help to implement it. Under Lincoln, the government instituted no educational or economic assistance for the freedmen. Nor were provisions made for granting the vote to Negroes. This was a privilege denied the blacks in most Northern states, a fact to which Southerners pointed mockingly. "If it's wrong for 'niggers' to vote up North, then it's wrong down here as well!" a prominent Southerner told a New York newspaperman who had asked his opinion on Negro suffrage. "When you give them full civil rights, then come and talk to us; otherwise you're spouting Yankee hypocrisy!"

The most Lincoln did about helping to get the vote for the Negro was to suggest mildly that perhaps some colored men should be rewarded with the franchise. "Let it be given . . . to the most intelligent and especially those who have fought in our ranks," Lincoln said. He made haste to reassure the Southerners that the states should have full authority to decide who could or could not vote.

When Arkansas, Louisiana and Tennessee, seeking readmission to the Union, adopted constitutions in which the vote was limited to white male citizens, Lincoln did not think this reason enough to withhold recognition from their newly created loyal governments. He believed that white men would never give the Negro full civil rights; nor did he press them to do so. It must be stressed that Lincoln's main concern was not with the Negro, but with saving the Union.

As the war raged on to its conclusion, Lincoln's recon-

struction plan boiled down to a policy aimed at swift restoration of rebel states to the Union with a minimum of
federal involvement in their internal affairs. Most white
Confederates could expect amnesty and the power to set
up loyal governments.

With few exceptions, even ardent Rebels could apply
for a pardon and probably get one without difficulty.
The leaders of Confederacy, Lincoln earnestly desired,
should be allowed to escape the country and live out
their days in some foreign land, exiled from the United
States.

Portrayed by history as an idealistic dreamer, Lincoln
actually was a no-nonsense realist. He foresaw much that
happened in the South during the years of the Reconstruction period when, for a time after Lincoln's death,
Yankee humanitarians and Radical Republicans almost
brought about a revolution in the South.

The main impact of that upheaval was on the relationship between whites and blacks. Under Radical Reconstruction, Southern Negroes tasted political equality for
a few years, although they were still treated as social
and economic inferiors. But, until the 1870s, Negroes
voted, held office (two were elected to the United States
Senate), received free educations and glimpsed the road
to a better life, a richer existence in a genuinely democratic society.

But Radical rule was toppled, the Conservatives took
over and the struggle for Negro civil liberties was nearly
abandoned, to remain dormant for nearly a hundred
years, until it was renewed in the 1950s and 1960s.

As Lincoln had feared, the Radical Reconstruction program so embittered white Southerners that they rejected the Republican party. For decades they voted a straight Democratic ticket, to create the political bloc known as the "Solid South," with Democrats in full, unquestioned control and Republicans almost nonexistent.

V

THERE WAS REJOICING over the length and breadth of the Union on April 9, 1865. On that day, General Robert E. Lee surrendered the Army of Northern Virginia to General Ulysses S. Grant at Appomattox Court House, and the long, costly war was ended. No more would Americans kill Americans on the battlefield. The war was done, the guns silent, and church bells pealed joyfully across the land.

In the war-ravaged South, with its barren fields and fire-blackened homes, farmlands lay desolate and bleak. In towns and cities and villages, the defeated people wept with relief. No longer would young men come stumbling home, blinded and maimed. The Southerners had fought hard for a Cause many now realized was a hollow one, built on illusion.

Many had known they were fighting for a way of life which had no place in the late nineteenth century; yet they had fought with courage and with honor.

But slavery was finished. Only the big planters owned

many slaves; only about 10,000 planters had 50 or more. Possibly 6,000,000 of the 8,000,000 white Southerners owned no slaves at all. The average "mudsill" Southerner was happy to be able to feed just his own kin, not to mention a black. What if the rich had lost their slaves? With all the wrack and ruin, few could have afforded them much longer. Most white Southerners felt that the blacks would come begging for work, for a piece of bread, because they weren't used to being on their own. The field-hands and house servants were like children and had to be looked after. So the whites felt they had nothing to fear from them.

And with Mr. Lincoln in Washington, a man could take the oath of allegiance, forget the war, roll up his sleeves and start working to bring the land back to life. The times ahead would be tough, but if a man bent his back to the plow, the earth would be green again.

So the lean and weary Southern soldiers trudged back along the dusty roads, ready to face another kind of war, a struggle for economic, social and political survival. It was to be a pitiless battle which fed bigotry, prejudices and bitterness.

Demagogues and racists stirred hatreds; white men persecuted black with a callousness and cruelty seldom known. And as a free man, the hapless Negro became the victim of an oppression even more crushing than he had known under slavery. It was a time that left to the United States a heritage of complex problems still unsolved a century later because they had been left unresolved.

Even while the nation was still rejoicing over the surrender at Appomattox, tragedy rocked it. On the evening of April 14, Good Friday, Abraham Lincoln attended the theater, and while he chuckled at the comedy being enacted onstage, he was murdered by an assassin. The killer, John Wilkes Booth, an actor, made his escape in the confusion that followed the shooting. (He was caught some days later in a barn at Fort Royal, Virginia, and shot dead.)

The assassination thrust the country into new turmoil. Lincoln was succeeded as Chief Executive by Vice-President Andrew Johnson, a man of humble origins, who had risen to high office through grit, determination and will power. Johnson's term in the White House was to be marked by endless controversy and political squabbling.

On Saturday, April 15, 1865, the day after Lincoln's assassination, while a chilling rain fell on Washington, a small group of Radical Republicans held a meeting at the Capitol. Tolling church bells, the same bells that had pealed so merrily after Appomattox, were sounding a knell for the fallen President. The bright bunting that had bedecked Washington had been replaced by draperies of mourning. But the men attending the meeting had not come to grieve over Lincoln's death; they had come to plan the political strategy for the crucial times ahead.

Among those present were key members of the powerful congressional Committee on the Conduct of the War, men vigorously opposed to Lincoln's reconstruction plans. Leading Radicals such as Senator Ben Wade, Senator Zachariah Chandler and Representative George Julian denounced any "soft" peace for the South. They feared that a policy of that sort would permit former rebel leaders to regain prewar political and economic power.

With Lincoln dead, the Radicals were determined not to let Johnson follow his predecessor's program for the South. They approached this task with some confidence, fairly certain that Johnson sympathized with them. Although the new President was a Southerner, hailing from Tennessee, and before the war had been a Democrat (Johnson claimed still to be a Democrat), his past actions and recent statements about the rebellion convinced the Radicals that he was on their side.

They had good reason to believe this of him. Like his idol, Andrew Jackson, another Tennessean, Johnson was an ardent Unionist—"Union above all" was his slogan. To prove that this was no hollow credo when his native state seceded in 1860, Johnson, serving as a U.S. Senator from Tennessee repudiated his state's secession declaration and kept his Senate seat. As a member of the Committee on the Conduct of the War, Johnson had worked well with the Radicals. In 1862, after Union troops had overrun much of Tennessee, Lincoln appointed him military governor of the recaptured state.

Johnson did this job so well that he was picked as Lincoln's running mate on the 1864 wartime coalition ticket. The fiery Tennessean's campaign highly pleased the Radicals. Johnson flayed Southern "aristocrats" and demanded a "harsh retribution" against them. "I say the traitor has ceased to be a citizen," he thundered. "In joining the rebellion he has become a public enemy." No one was more vehement than he in calling for stern punishment of rebels. "Treason must be made odious. Traitors must be punished and impoverished," he cried.

Coming to office on the heels of a murdered chief, Johnson mirrored the bitterness rampant in the North. He loosed verbal blasts at the Southerners and their leaders, even accusing them of plotting Lincoln's assassination. Johnson offered rewards for the capture of Jefferson Davis as well as John Wilkes Booth and his accomplices. There seemed no doubt that he was anxious to try some Confederate leaders for treason. He also evinced interest in the 1862 Confiscation Act as a means of breaking up large Southern estates and made clear his commitment to total abolition of slavery.

There was nothing about Andrew Johnson's attitude which even vaguely hinted that Rebels might expect compassion, generosity or softness from him. Only ten days after Lincoln's death, Senator Chandler expressed satisfaction with him. "Johnson . . . is as radical as I am, fully up to the mark. If he has good men around him, there will be no danger in the future," the Senator stated confidently.

VI

DURING THE EARLY DAYS of his administration, Johnson was surrounded by the sort of "good" men Chandler had in mind. The President's former associates in the Committee on the Conduct of the War became his unofficial advisers and Johnson met with them frequently. He heard their ideas, apparently with sympathy, rarely saying anything, but listening raptly.

After one such session, Senator Wade shook his hand warmly. "Mr. President, we have faith in you, complete faith. By the gods, there'll be no trouble now in running the government."

To this Johnson responded earnestly, "Senator, I believe treason must be made infamous and traitors must be impoverished." He had said that many times before, but his voice rang so sincerely that the pat phrase rang fresh and new.

The Radicals had every reason to assume Johnson was their man. They were convinced he would repudiate the state governments Lincoln had recognized, reorganize

the Cabinet, bring to trial for treason a number of leading rebels, and either delay political reconstruction of the
South until Congress reconvened in December, or else
call a special session to debate the matter. A Radical
newspaper, the New York *Independent*, wrote glowingly
of him:

> Providence has trained . . . a Southern loyalist in the
> midst of traitors, a Southern democrat in the midst of
> aristocrats . . . to be lifted at last to the presidency of
> the United States that he might be charged with the
> duty of meting out punishment to these self-same as-
> sassins of the United States.

In the beginning all was sweetness and light between
Andrew Johnson and Congress. Yet, three years later,
that harmony dissolved into discord. The same Radicals
who hardly could find enough words to praise him suffered the same shortage in damning Johnson. For the first
time in American history impeachment proceedings were
brought in Congress against a President. The attempt to
unseat Johnson failed by only one vote.

How had such a dramatic turnabout taken place?

The spectacular change resulted partly from Johnson's
altered stand on reconstruction; as time went by he abandoned the Radical approach to it for a Conservative one.
But that was not the only reason. The President's tact-
lessness in dealing with Congress, together with a sense
of stubborn independence, an inability to compromise,
and overweening faith in his own judgment, helped create the crisis.

Another contributing factor was the failure of the Radicals to understand Johnson. They mistakenly thought that he was entirely on their side, but the area of agreement between the President and the Radicals had been a slim one from the outset. That this did not become immediately apparent stemmed from Johnson's lack of candor in dealing with the Radicals about most problems in general, and reconstruction specifically.

Johnson seemed cooperative with the Radicals to a point, but their social and political aims for the reconstructed South went beyond his. The Radicals intended using federal power to gain civil and political rights for Negroes. Many Radicals hoped to keep certain war legislation in effect to help business; laws such as the protective tariff were favored by Northern commercial interests. As a group, the Radicals believed that "what benefitted business, benefitted the American."

Despite their tag, the Radicals were radical only because they backed certain domestic reforms opposed by the rest of the Republican party. But that was where their radicalism ended. Radicals supported Big Business and envisioned a grand future for manufacturing, railroads, mining and many other mushrooming industries. Legislation that favored business was favored by the Radicals. It was only on slavery and the Negro question that they talked idealism. In their desire to do away with slavery and wipe out Southern planter aristocracy, some of them seemed almost zealots.

Andrew Johnson was not convinced that he wanted the Negro to gain full civil and political rights, nor did he care to smooth the road for a rapidly rising American capitalism. Neither Republican, Radical nor Conservative, Johnson did not welcome the social and economic changes emerging from the Civil War. In an era of expanding railroads, growing corporations and commercialized farming, Johnson believed in the independent farmer and artisan and regarded cities as symbols of moral decay.

Although he fervently loved the Union, Johnson clung to old-fashioned concepts of states rights in preference to a highly centralized federal government. To him, the principles of Thomas Jefferson and Andrew Jackson were guidance enough for the nation. He felt that the Democratic party, despite misguided Southern leaders, remained the best custodian of the national destiny.

A self-made man, Johnson took pride in his career. As a child in North Carolina, he had known great poverty and privation. While still a youth, lacking formal schooling, he had moved alone across the mountains to East Tennessee, a region of small farms and virtually no slavery. Settling in the village of Greenville, Johnson had established a tailor shop which brought him a comfortable income in return for hard work.

Aided by his wife, he had learned to read and write. He had entered politics as a Jacksonian Democrat and become the champion of poor farmers, working artisans and the underprivileged masses. A bitter foe of the rich, proud and affluent, he had once said, "Some day I will show the stuck-up aristocrats just who is running this country. A cheap, purse-proud set they are, not half as good as the man who earns his bread by the sweat of his brow."

His rise in politics had been meteoric, as he went from alderman to mayor of Greenville, then to the state legislature and to Congress for five terms. For two terms he had been governor of Tennessee and by 1857 had gone to the United States Senate.

Always fighting for the poor Southern white man, Johnson pictured himself the champion of the underdog. "The people need friends," he had said. "They have a great deal to bear." In Tennessee, Johnson was a true friend of the people. He fought for the common man and crusaded to win free, tax-supported public schools throughout the state. On the national scene, the ex-tailor continued to campaign for the poor. He backed the Homestead Act, which offered to a settler 160 acres of public land. Johnson felt this was the best way to end poverty. In a speech supporting the Act, he said:

> I want no miserable city rabble on the one hand; I want no pampered, bloated, corrupt aristocracy on the other; I want the middle portion of society to be built up and sustained. . . . Let us go on interesting men in becoming connected with the soil, . . . prevent their accumulation in the streets of your cities; and in doing this, dispense with the necessity of your pauper system.

Although siding with the people, Johnson was no abolitionist and had owned a few slaves himself. However, as a democrat, Johnson raised an odd objection to slavery. It was bad, he said, not because human bondage was evil, but because only the rich could afford to keep slaves. Once, in speaking of his hopes for bettering the life of the common man, Johnson declared fervently, "I wish to God every head of a family in the United States had one slave to take the drudgery of menial service off his family."

Like so many Southern advocates of democracy, Johnson's creed excluded Negroes; his was democracy for whites only. However, Johnson neither hated Negroes nor wished them harm. By 1864, he realized that slavery had to become a war casualty and willingly accepted this outcome. "The abolition of slavery," he said, "is right in itself . . . and by the emancipation of the slaves, we break down an odious and dangerous aristocracy."

On one point he seemed unwavering—his desire to destroy the Southern planter aristocracy. At the same time, he did not intend to let the newly rich Northern manufacturers, and industrialists, arrogant war-made capitalists, take over the postwar South. "I do not intend to see a Northern moneyed aristocracy replace the Southern landed aristocracy," he declared. "In the reborn, reconstructed South, the small man, the yeoman farmer, the so called 'mudsill' must hold the reins of power."

Like some latter-day Robin Hood, Johnson meant to take from the rich and give to the poor. He railed against the protective tariff as an unjust burden on the people, since it raised the price of imported manufactured goods. He denounced the sale of timber and mineral rights in public lands to private corporations as a violation of the 1862 Homestead Act. "Public lands are a national trust,"

he proclaimed, "set apart and held for the general welfare . . . and not to be bestowed as a special privilege
on a favored class." Thundering and orating, fuming and
fretting, President Johnson aimed blows at the Southern
"lords of the manor" and the "Yankee masters of capital"
in the cause of the small farmer, the tiller of the soil, the
"hewers of wood and haulers of water," whom he called
the backbone of the nation and "God's chosen people."

Time after time, the farmers had been betrayed by
powerful interests, first, by Hamilton and the Federalist
commercial aristocracy until Jefferson returned the government to the "dirt farmer," then by the bankers, until
Jackson smashed them. After that came the wealthy
Southern planters whom Andrew Johnson had fought all
his political career. Now, after the long and dreadful war,
he would help his beloved "mudsills" gain their rightful
place in the Southern sun.

VII

FROM THE VANTAGE OF THE WHITE HOUSE, President Johnson was in a position to win the long fight he had been waging for his people. In this time of political reconstruction, he would raise them to power in the New South. The instrument through which to do this was a strong, reorganized Democratic party, purged of its traitorous wartime leaders. With the small farmers in the saddle, the South soon would become a democratic agrarian society, a veritable paradise.

Unfortunately, this vision put Johnson at cross-purposes with Radical Republicans from the industrial Northeast. They had a different concept of paradise: an industrialized South, a capitalistic South with railroads and factories, mills and shops, a young giant of industry where hordes of workers toiled at machines instead of behind the plow. The burgeoning corporations, trusts and monopolies saw in the South a virgin territory for expansion and this the Radicals decided would bring salvation to that semi-feudal region.

The Radicals also had a program for the Southern Negro. They were determined to see that he got the vote and used it to vote Republican. Unless this happened, they were convinced, Southern and Northern Democrats would form a powerful coalition to sweep the Republicans out of power. This could be counteracted only by a massive Republican vote in the South—and the only ones the Radicals felt they could count on to deliver the necessary plurality were the former slaves.

It stood to reason that merely securing the vote for the Negro was not enough. He had to have protection as well, the same recourse to the law as his white neighbor. This the Radicals also supported—although they by no means advocated social or even economic equality for Negroes.

The differences between the Radicals' program and Johnson's inevitably led to a clash. There were other elements as well, some of them personal. Unlike Lincoln, President Johnson was not able to win over his subordinates with sophisticated wit, homespun humor and shrewd political tactics. Johnson could not master himself, let alone others; he was quick-tempered and heavy-handed, a man made bitter by his humble beginnings and early suffering.

He lacked ease, grace and self-confidence; he tried to overcome these shortcomings with a stiff, unbending stubbornness which he believed was a substitute for resolution. Easily angered and given to making indiscreet statements, Johnson was a mark for nimble-tongued foes who goaded and baited him. Instead of ignoring their barbs, Johnson replied in wrath and often made a fool of himself.

The first indications that the Radicals were no longer beguiled by Johnson came after the President stopped threatening the Rebels and got down to the business of reconstruction.

Sensing that time was of the utmost importance, the Radicals urged the President to call a special session of Congress and move swiftly. Carl Schurz, writing from the South to Senator Charles Sumner early in May 1865, said:

> If we only make a vigorous start in the right direction the problem will be easily solved. But if too much latitude is given to the mischievous elements in the South for the next few weeks, it will be exceedingly difficult to set matters right again.

Johnson needed no prodding from the Radicals or anyone else. He was anxious to launch a reconstruction program and told this to a Radical delegation, which left a meeting with the Chief Executive in high spirits. "We have Johnson in our hip pocket!" a Radical boasted. "He's all ours!"

However, the President belonged to no one but himself and soon showed it by issuing a series of executive proclamations and public statements that left the Radicals gasping. Everything Johnson now said and did was a reversal of his previous position.

Like Lincoln before him, Johnson suddenly revealed his belief that reconstruction should be under the jurisdiction of the executive, and not the legislative branch of the government. He refused to honor the request for a special session of Congress, nor would he delay launching a reconstruction program until the regular session in December. Instead, he intended to put his plan into operation so that when Congress convened he could present it with a neat package labeled "Reconstruction."

Wade, Chandler and other Radicals had deluded themselves into believing that Johnson would reshuffle his Cabinet, replacing Conservatives with Radicals. They quickly learned their mistake. The President kept all of Lincoln's Cabinet members. No longer did he meet with the Radicals and listen to their advice. He simply ignored them and refused all their requests for a conference. Evidently the President proposed to go it alone, consulting neither the Radicals, his Cabinet, nor anyone else on what course to follow.

It was one thing for Lincoln, who had been elected to office and had popular support, to snub Congress. But Johnson's behavior toward the legislators was sheer folly; he had attained the post of Chief Executive through chance, not by election. Small wonder that the Radicals belittled him with the title, "His Accidency the President."

But Johnson long before had learned to ride roughshod over adversaries. To the total displeasure of the Radicals, he announced that, with some modifications, he would follow Lincoln's reconstruction plan.

On May 9, 1865, the President made his first move, recognizing Francis H. Pierpont as governor of Virginia and legalizing the state government. Three weeks later, on

May 29, 1865, Johnson, in two proclamations, outlined his reconstruction policy for the South.

In the first he ordered an oath of allegiance to be administered to the mass of Southerners; those taking it would automatically be granted full amnesty and pardon, and the restoration of all property, except slaves, unless confiscation proceedings were underway. Swearing to the oath gave a former rebel immunity from prosecution for treason or conspiracy or under the provisions of the Confiscation Act.

However, 14 classes of former Confederates were not covered by this generous and sweeping oath. During the war Johnson had said: "Many humble men, the peasantry and yeomanry of the South, who have been decoyed, or perhaps driven into rebellion, may look forward with reasonable hope for an amnesty. But the intelligent and influential leaders must suffer."

Included in the exempt groups were various categories of Confederate civil and military officers, as might be expected. In addition Johnson listed an extra category, which exposed his personal feelings. Men who had backed the rebellion and whose taxable property was assessed at $20,000 or more, were barred from taking the oath. Here Johnson behaved as a class-conscious plebeian at grips with his old antagonists—the rich. When a group of Virginians protested this clause, Johnson coldly told them, "You know perfectly well it was the wealthy men of the South who dragooned the people into secession."

He meant to bar the aristocracy from playing any role

in reconstruction. This was a way to put "mudsills" into positions of political power. Without pardons, the large property owners would be politically impotent, unable to vote, hold office or assert influence in government. However, their situation was not entirely hopeless. Men ineligible for pardon under the May 29 proclamation could petition the President for a special pardon. Johnson gave assurances that each case would be treated on its own merits at a fair and impartial hearing. Many prominent Southerners were quick to take advantage of this, and received pardons.

This part of Johnson's plan seemed to defeat his whole purpose; on the one hand, he had vowed to crush the ruling classes of the South; on the other, he had given them a reentry into public life. He did so because he was not basically a tyrant but a fair and honest man. Also he was convinced that the average Southerner never again would rely upon the people who had led the South to ruin.

This misplaced faith in the judgment and sagacity of poor white farmers brought near disaster to Johnson and the nation as a whole; soon many of the old leaders were back in the saddle, elected to important posts by the "mudsill" class Johnson had worked so hard and so long to raise from poverty to power.

VIII

THE SECOND PRESIDENTIAL PROCLAMATION of May 29
described the procedure to be followed in forming loyal
state governments. (Virginia, Arkansas, Louisiana and
Tennessee were not affected by the decree. They already
had administrations recognized by Lincoln and later by
Johnson.) According to the proclamation, the President
would appoint a military governor for each former Confederate state, whose duty it was to call a state convention and supervise the election of delegates to that body.
The only persons permitted either to vote or to stand for
election were those so qualified in 1860 and who had
taken the oath of allegiance. The convention would draw
up procedures for a permanent government, after which
an election would be held for governor, state legislators
and members of Congress.

Once this had been accomplished and the state government had passed resolutions denouncing secession,
repudiating all Confederate debts and ratifying the Thirteenth Amendment, the reconstruction for the state was

to be considered complete. Then martial law was to be revoked by the order of the President, federal troops withdrawn and the state again to be considered an equal member of the Union.

As the frustrated and fuming Radicals looked on, Johnson set his reconstruction program in motion during the summer of 1865. By late autumn, the conventions had concluded their business. State elections had been held and newly elected loyal governments installed throughout the South.

Affairs seemed to have gone smoothly enough for Johnson, at least on the surface; when Congress reconvened in December 1865, ten of the 11 Confederate states had complied with his reconstruction program. (The remaining state, Texas, finally accomplished it in spring, 1866.) At a joint session of Congress, Johnson announced to the members that the process of reconstruction—or restoration, as he called it—was over. The Southerners, he said, were once again "in the fold." The states had resumed their proper places in the Union. Federal courts, custom houses and post offices were operating normally. It was incumbent on Congress to seat Southern representatives and senators and welcome them "as brothers," the President said. Concluding his report, Johnson remarked, "The aspect of affairs is more promising than, in view of all the circumstances, could well have been expected." To the audience, he seemed pleased.

But his satisfaction soon curdled. The Radicals in Congress balked at Johnson's role in Reconstruction. If he had expected Congress to accept his program as an accomplished fact, the President was bitterly disappointed. The Radicals refused to yield an inch and fought a grueling political battle with him, a bitter clash which shook the nation to its core.

Johnson had foreseen the possibility of this development and was ready for it; what he could neither foresee nor believe, when it happened, was the outcome of his long-cherished scheme to give the poor farmers the upper hand in the South. His attempt to create an agrarian Utopia there under the leadership of the lower classes failed, although Johnson refused to concede it either publicly or privately.

He did not succeed because the people upon whom he had counted through the years rejected him. He never had fully understood them or what they really wanted.

All his life, Johnson had believed that Southern poor whites were exploited and victimized by the landed gentry and longed for new leaders to arise and rescue them.

According to the President, the aristocrats had plotted and carried out secession and rebellion against the people's will. It had been a "rich man's war and a poor man's fight," Johnson believed; and now, with slaveholders and landowners beaten, their policies discredited, he thought the "mudsills" would rise *en masse* against them. From the ranks of the deprived and exploited would come strong, energetic men dedicated to the creation of a new South without a haughty aristocracy, a South where humble men ruled and lived in pride and dignity.

The only trouble with Johnson's ambitions was that his estimate of the existing situation was distorted. He had

misinterpreted the relationship between impoverished
farmer and rich planter. In the past, there had been tensions between the groups. The poor farmers resented and
envied the planters with their fine homes, slaves, thor-
oughbred horses, broad fields and high living.

It was a far cry, indeed, from the mansion on the hill-
top to the mean farm cabin in the bottomland. The dirt
farmer wrenched a meager livelihood from reluctant
earth. His children went barefoot and unschooled; his
wife was weary with toil. She wore calico, while the
planter's lady had silks and satins. The "mudsill," standing meekly before the lord of the manor, head bowed,
hat in hand, was treated with a disdain reserved for
slaves and underlings. Only his white skin made him su-
perior to the blacks; although no slave, he was in bondage to the land, always in debt and generally hungry.
Uncomfortably aware of his lack of learning, often wholly
illiterate, the ordinary farmer regarded with awe the
smooth, self-confident planters.

To them, the well-dressed aristocrat represented success on every level. If they hated the planter, they also
admired him; and nobody could shake their confidence in
his leadership. They followed him willingly. How could
he be wrong? He knew everything. Wasn't he rich and
important?

If certain undemocratic political practices were prevalent in the prewar South, most unpropertied, non-
slaveholding whites had the right to vote without coer-
cion from the planters.

The aristocrats employed accepted political tactics to

win and hold power. They ruled by ballot, not force. Their wealth, education and social position won for them the confidence and the support of the masses.

Contrary to Johnson's ideas, few Southerners had been reluctant to secede from the Union. On the contrary, most poor whites in the Confederate states wholeheartedly endorsed secession. Nor had defeat in war shaken their confidence in the old leadership; in fact, the people were bound to it more strongly than ever by the fire of battle.

A Union officer, writing from the South, in 1865, noted: "Everywhere that I went, I found the . . . Southerner still under the domination of his ancient leaders." The 1865 elections bore out this observation. Although small farmers did make political gains in certain regions, such as Tennessee, where Unionists won complete control, the picture was changed only slightly; in most places planters and former Confederate leaders easily captured the Johnson governments, to the President's dismay.

A number of newly elected governors and legislators wore their weatherbeaten Confederate campaign hats and bragged of wartime exploits. Few even bothered to take the oath of allegiance required by Johnson. Many remained in categories excluded from the general amnesty.

Despite these restrictions, they stood for office and won handily, often over pro-Union opponents, whom all "true" Southerners despised as traitors. Those having Union sentiment were known as "scalawags." Yankees who went South after the war were labeled "carpetbaggers." (It was claimed that they carried all their belongings in a carpetbag and had come down only to victimize Southerners.)

Flouting Johnson's proclamation, known secessionists were placed in office. Governor James Orr of South Carolina had been a Confederate senator. Mississippi's governor, Benjamin G. Humphreys, had been a brigadier general in the Rebel army. Nor were they the only ones; most of those elected to Congress had been important military, naval or civil officers in the Confederacy. The most prominent was Alexander H. Stephens of Georgia, the Vice-President of the Confederacy, who won a seat in the United States Senate.

Johnson was upset by the elections. He faced a ticklish situation; the Southerners had defied him by electing men to whom amnesty had been denied. The President could have checked the reviving rebel spirit by declaring the elections void, ordering new ones and backing up his proclamation with troops.

Johnson had not allowed time for poor Southerners and those with Union sympathies to develop leaders capable of assuming political responsibility. But instead of rallying Southern Unionists, he betrayed them by announcing that he would issue a pardon to any Rebel who asked for one.

There was a great rush for presidential clemency. A former Confederate colonel was appointed Clerk of Pardons to speed the process. Southern governors, legislators, congressmen, senators, ex-officers and Confederate luminaries received pardons without question. So-called pardon brokers charged applicants $150 to $200 for a guaranteed pardon. It was a profitable racket. By September 1865, pardons were being granted at the rate of more than 100 a day.

In the South, bands of self-styled "Regulators" were formed. Recruited from among former Confederate soldiers, these gangs roved the countryside to enforce "law and order." Actually, they persecuted pro-Union men and militant Negroes, beating, torturing and even killing them. Homes were burned. Shots sounded in the night. Terror swept the hinterlands as the Regulators rode forth to fan the embers of rebellion and crush dissenters. Carpetbaggers were among the chief targets of these night riders, especially teachers and others who had come to help freed Negroes.

The old order in the South had not given way to the new. Except for its defeat in war, the South still clung to antebellum social and political lines.

IX

COMMITTED AS HE WAS to a policy of presidential Reconstruction, Johnson could only be true to himself and continue along the path he had chosen. His major concern was not the Negro, or his "social revolution," but the restoration of the Union. This led him to take steps which seem contradictory, but grew out of his dedication to his principles. For instance, after first refusing amnesty to the Southern aristocrats, he granted them full pardon.

Historians have been hard put to discover Johnson's motives. Some feel that his firm belief in democracy allowed him no course but to pardon the Confederate leaders once the people had voted them into office. Others believe Johnson was convinced Radical Reconstruction might rekindle rebellion in the South and eventually lead to another civil war.

It also was said that Johnson hated the upcoming Yankee capitalists more than he did Southern aristocrats and discerned in the planter class a political force to thwart the growing influence of Northern businessmen in the South.

It is more likely that, though he had publicly advocated class struggle and social change, Johnson was a conservative at heart. When the hour of revolution arrived, he shrank from the prospect of turmoil and let the planters win. A few cynical observers thought Johnson had his eye on the 1868 presidential campaign and wanted all the Southern support he could muster.

Johnson's motives matter less than the result, which was that the South remained in the clutches of its traditional leaders. The President's attitude softened toward his adversaries. No longer did he rant that treason must be made odious and traitors punished. On the contrary, he now said: "I never expected to keep out all who were excluded from the amnesty, or even a large number of them, but I intended they should sue for pardon, and so realize the enormity of their crime."

In response to this Southerners flocked to the President, seeking and receiving pardons. But they were neither repentant nor humble. Nor did they regard past deeds as crimes. The planter politicians emerged triumphant from the wreckage of the Confederacy. Once more they ruled the roost. The Southerners made a shambles of Johnson's reconstruction plans. They beat him at his own game—politics. Because he had to defend himself against attacks by the Radicals, Johnson was forced into an alliance with the Southern planter-politicians—the only allies he had left. He refused to concede failure. Such a concession would have been an invitation for Congress to take over the task of reconstruction.

In his report to Congress, Johnson claimed all was going well in the South. His program was a complete success. The men who headed the state governments were loyal and honorable. Southerners, as a whole, had accepted the war's outcome and harbored no grudges against the North. Abolition was a reality. According to Johnson, slavery no longer existed in the South and the former slaves were being fairly treated by their recent masters.

Stability and tranquillity were flourishing and these blissful conditions had been swiftly achieved without undue difficulty.

Had all this been true, Johnson probably could have forced Congress to recognize the state governments set up under his plan. But the actual conditions in the South differed greatly from his description of them. Turbulence and disorder reigned. Violence rose daily against Negroes and their white sympathizers, while law-enforcement officers stood idly by. The Johnson-approved state governments failed to provide safeguards. Only federal troops gave security, but their numbers had been so reduced as to render available forces ineffective.

The Radicals greeted Johnson's message to Congress with scepticism. Led by Representative Thaddeus Stevens of Pennsylvania and Senator Charles Sumner of Massachusetts, the Radicals contradicted the President on almost every point. The Southerners who ran the state governments were rebels at heart, Radical spokesmen claimed. The rebellion still burned in the Confederacy. Northerners were persecuted and the Negro once again was being driven into slavery, Stevens insisted.

Several investigative delegations were sent to the South to report on conditions there. Johnson dispatched General Ulysses S. Grant and a pro-administration newsman, Benjamin C. Truman, on a tour through the "reconstructed" states. Their reports pleased the President. Grant noted that "the mass of thinking men in the South accept the present situation . . . in good faith." Truman observed in April 1866 that "the great, substantial and prevailing element . . . is more loyal now than at the end of the war."

However, Carl Schurz, another presidential investigator, offered a diametrically opposed opinion to these views. He warned that "the lid will soon blow off. . . . The South is a volcano about to erupt." (In April and May 1866, Schurz was borne out by violent riots in Memphis, Tennessee, and New Orleans, Louisiana, during which rampaging mobs killed scores of Negroes.)

Evidently the Southerners both resented and refused to accept Yankee domination. Several states failed to admit secession was wrong. Forced by military defeat to comply, they repealed, but never repudiated, secession. In Arkansas, the Johnson-approved state government voted pensions for Conferderate veterans, while Mississippi would not ratify the Thirteenth Amendment. And there rose to prominence a type of Southern politician whose chief asset was Yankee-baiting and to whom "Dixie," not "The Star-Spangled Banner," was the national anthem.

By present-day standards, the greatest failure of Johnson's program was the total inaction in regard to the Negroes. In the early war years, the President had adhered to Lincoln's resettlement project as the solution of the Negro problem. By 1865, he had come to realize that the Negro was a permanent part of the American scene. Despite this conclusion, the President's Reconstruction plan had no special requirements for Southern recognition of Negro rights. Johnson went no further than demanding that slavery be abolished. He did not believe the federal government had the power to legislate educational, civil, political or social benefits for Negroes and most of Congress, including Radicals, agreed with him. These questions, he maintained, remained within the province of the individual states, which was a strict interpretation of the Constitution.

Johnson vaguely supported the right of Negroes to vote and once suggested to the governor of Mississippi that Negroes who met literacy and property requirements should be given this privilege, if only to "disarm" the Radicals who were "wild upon Negro franchise."

But Negro suffrage was not a condition for recognition of a state government. Clarifying his stand on the matter, Johnson stated:

> My position as President . . . is different from what it would be were I in Tennessee. . . . There I should try to introduce Negro suffrage gradually. . . . It would not do to let the Negro have universal suffrage now. . . . It would breed a war of the races.

Johnson did not back Negro suffrage, mainly because he was convinced that former slaveholders and planters would control the votes of these "helpless and dependent people." The President's lack of empathy with Negro desires for equality, and his failure to give adequate federal protection for them, drove the ex-slaves straight into the Radical camp.

The fact that the state governments he had declared legal stood on a "white supremacy" platform did not disturb Johnson. His indifference was not unusual. Most states of the Union were formed on a "lily white" basis—only five Northern states allowed Negroes to vote—and of these, just one—Massachusetts—gave Negroes full civil and political equality.

In his inaugural address, Governor Benjamin Humphreys of Mississippi promised: "Ours is, and shall ever be, a government of white men."

The state convention held in New Orleans, Louisiana, proclaimed:

> We hold this to be a Government of White People, made and to be perpetuated for the exclusive political benefit of the White Race. . . . The People of African descent cannot be considered as citizens of the United States.

So it went in one "reconstructed" state after another. The Negro, released from slavery, had still not lost his chains; he was shackled by the color of his skin. The long-awaited Day of Jubilee had come, but for him it brought neither liberation nor enlightenment. Denied human rights as a slave, he was to be denied political rights as a freeman.

X

CARL SCHURZ, in his report from the South mentioned earlier, revealed that whites feared education for the Negro even more than they did the possibility of his voting. He wrote:

> The popular prejudice is almost as bitterly set against the Negro's having the advantage of education as it was when he was a slave. . . . Hundreds of times I have heard the old assertation repeated . . . "learning will spoil the nigger for work." Another, most singular notion still holds a potent sway over the minds of the masses—it is, that the elevation of the blacks will be the degradation of the whites.

Schurz aroused little interest with his comments about Negro education and the Southern attitudes toward it. Such views were prevalent throughout the United States at the time. Neither President Johnson nor anyone else cared about federal aid to education for Negroes *or* whites—whether in the North *or* in the South. This thinking was typical of the era—the federal government simply did not get involved in matters such as education; in fact, few states did and in many areas there were no state-supported schools.

Clearly President Johnson thought the federal government had done enough in emancipating the slaves. Plans to lift the Negro's economic status also were nonexistent. As in the past, the future was bleak for the Negro. He was forced to stay an illiterate and unskilled agricultural worker—a veritable human beast of burden. A postwar Texas politician, speaking at a meeting, said of the Negroes:

> I concede them nothing but the station of hewers of wood and drawers of water. . . . They aren't fit for anything better.

This was a feeling, not limited to the South. In the industrial North, white mechanics and laborers refused to work with Negroes; the worst, lowest-paid jobs were relegated to the blacks. Trade unions would not accept them as members. They were barred from many skills and trades.

But up North, the Negro was not the only object of discrimination. Immigrants flocking to the United States from Ireland, Germany, Hungary and Italy also were treated unfairly and harshly; scorn and abuse were heaped upon them. But the "greenhorns"—post-Civil War slang for immigrants—had an advantage over the Negro; at least they were white. Succeeding generations were assimilated into the mainstream of society, but the black man was forever branded undesirable by his white neighbors.

Prevalent, too, was the belief that Negroes were racially inferior to whites. A leading Virginian, noted for his humanitarian work, declared:

> I do not believe that the . . . Negro will ever have the persistence of purpose, or the energy, or the intellectual vigor to rise to anything like intellectual equality with the white man. . . . The Negro is proud to call you master. . . . In the name of humanity, let him do so.

It also was commonly believed that Negroes would not work unless compelled, in some fashion, to do so. A prominent Southerner remarked that, in the old days, the whip induced a black to work. "You can't whip him anymore," he said. "But you can pass laws to make him work."

Throughout the South, such laws were passed. Known as Black Codes, they regulated the conduct of a Negro's life. According to Carl Schurz, these Codes "were a striking embodiment of the idea that, although the former owner had lost his individual right of property in the former slave, the blacks at large now belong to the whites at large."

In other words, the Black Codes placed the Negro somewhere between slavery and freedom. They covered every aspect of his daily existence, marking a narrow path for the Negro to tread. In these Codes, a groundwork was laid for complete segregation of the races in public facilities; interracial marriages were forbidden; Negroes were prohibited from serving on juries or even testifying against whites.

No Negro could accept any employment except agricultural work unless he had a special license. Unemployed Negroes were liable to arrest as vagrants. They were then either auctioned off or hired out for a year to landowners who would pay their fines.

In some states, Negroes were required to make contracts with landowners during the first ten days of January; once made, the contracts were effective for a year. After the year had elapsed, no Negro could leave his place of employment without the employer's permission. If a Negro refused to work for his employer, he might be arrested and put to forced labor on public works without pay until he went back to his boss.

The South, in its need to create a dependable labor force, was tying the Negro to his job. All over the South Negro leaders saw the Black Codes as a return to bondage and pleaded with Congress to rescue them from their plight. A Northern Congressman warned Mississippi, where the Codes were especially severe, that he would see the state "turned into a frog pond" before allowing slavery to be reestablished.

Many Southerners were stunned and shocked by the Codes; a leading Mississippi planter called them "amazingly arrogant and stupid." Eventually, many provisions in the Black Codes were either modified or thrown out by military authorities on the scene.

President Johnson obliquely defended the Codes. On

December 18, 1865, he referred to these enactments in a
special message to the Senate, calling them

> measures to confer upon freedmen . . . the privileges
> which are essential to their comfort, protection and se-
> curity. . . . Problems are naturally to be expected from
> the great and sudden changes between the races. But
> systems are gradually developing themselves under
> which the freedman will receive the protection to which
> he is justly entitled . . . and by means of his labor,
> make himself a useful and independent member of the
> community in which he has a home.

The apparent collapse of Johnson's Reconstruction
program threw the whole business into the hands of
Congress and created an unpleasant situation for the
President. From a dream of turning the South into a
"paradise" for the small farmer, his program had become
a means through which the Southern "establishment"—
the landlords and planters—were enabled to put a form
of bondage on their black workers. President Johnson's
Reconstruction policy had enabled them to do this. In
a sense, he was the best friend conservative Southerners
ever had. He had done more for them than their own
leaders, who had only brought on the long war in which
the South had paid so heavily.

The Radical Republicans had refused to accept Johnson's way. They turned on the President with implacable
fury and prepared to launch a "genuine" reconstruction
by arming the federal government with full powers to
give Negro emancipation real meaning.

What followed gave birth to the long-accepted tradition that the Radicals caused the ugly race relations which sullied the South throughout the late nineteenth and much of the twentieth centuries. Historians of the past claimed that, under Johnson's guidance, restoration of the Union was proceeding apace. A *modus vivendi* between whites and blacks was being worked out and would have succeeded, but all progress was wiped out by Radical intervention. Other, less partisan historians point out that the only accomplishment of Johnson Reconstruction was the reunification of the country. The Negro, although freed from slavery, benefitted in no other way under Johnson. At least the Radicals paid lip service to gaining basic civil rights for the ex-slaves.

The struggle between Andrew Johnson and Congress was reluctantly entered by both sides. Congress had not wanted to cross swords with the President and certainly, at the outset of his administration, the Radicals had given him all the support any Chief Executive could desire.

XI

By the time the Thirty-ninth Congress met, in December 1865, the last vestiges of goodwill toward Johnson were melting like snowdrifts in spring. The President's Reconstruction program was in full swing, causing an ever widening rift between the Radicals and Johnson. The Moderate Republicans, who held the balance of power in the Thirty-ninth Congress, tried vainly to maintain unity, but finally broke with the President over his "experiment" in reconstruction. Soon, the only congressional backing Johnson could muster came from the small Democratic minority and the handful of Conservative Republicans still holding seats.

Even after Johnson had started to organize state governments in the South, few Republicans were eager to break with him. A Radical spokesman, John Murray Forbes, spoke for his colleagues when, in August 1865, he said:

> My great hope lies in President Johnson's stubborn democracy. I have full faith in his hatred of the slave

aristocracy; and if he finds that under his experiment the oligarchy rears its head and begins to grasp the reins of power, I look to see him promptly resume the military power.

Forbes, like many others, regarded the President's program as an experiment. For many months, the Radicals, his most outspoken critics, were confident that he soon would see his mistakes and "chuck up the game." As one senator remarked:

> This thing going on down South . . . is a blunder. . . . Nobody in Congress approves it, but President Johnson is only experimenting, and we should give him the chance to try. . . . Once he realizes the idea can't work, he'll change tactics.

But such optimism could not long continue in the light of developments in the South. By the time Congress had assembled, most Radicals and many others of both House and Senate were ready to split with Johnson over the Reconstruction program. By early summer of 1865, several prominent Radicals, including Senators Sumner and Wade and Representative Stevens, already had done so. In July, Wade had written:

> We have in truth . . . lost the whole moral effect of our victories over the rebellion. . . . The golden opportunity for humiliating and destroying the Southern aristocracy has gone forever.

Yet, even as antagonisms were coming to the surface, Republican Moderates were striving to stave off the inevitable. A more subtle and skillful politician than the

President, a man of more tact and diplomacy possibly could have forestalled open conflict by winning over the Moderates and gaining a majority in Congress.

For this to happen, Johnson needed prudence and flexibility—qualities he sorely lacked. Also, the men who ran the Johnsonian governments in the Southern states needed to show some discretion. Instead, the President was uncompromising and tactless, while Southern leaders callously displayed contempt and indifference to public opinion in the North.

This combination of arrogance and hostility turned the Moderates from Johnson to the Radicals. The President had thrown away any influence he once had enjoyed with Congress. A contemporary journalist noted: "Andy Johnson couldn't win a vote in Congress today even if he offered a bill favoring Religion, Motherhood and Little Puppy Dogs."

By the summer of 1866, the Radicals completely dominated Congress and had sufficient strength to control the process of Reconstruction.

A long period of argument and debate raged in Washington; the President and his few faithful followers in Congress—those inclined to follow him though not altogether happy with his policies—battled furiously with words. Much of the verbal warfare was harsh, filled with name-calling, insults, character assassinations and false accusations. But there also was serious argument in the best parliamentary tradition.

Discussed were such subjects as the proper relationship between the legislative and executive branches; the point at which federal responsibility ended and that of the states began; and precisely how "soft" or "hard" the terms imposed on the South should be, now that Johnson's plan had to be scrapped.

One question cropped up time and again: Had the Southern states ever left the Union? Johnson argued that they had not, and hence it was necessary for them only to set up loyal governments to qualify for their former status.

Even the Radicals insisted that the states had left the Union. During the war the Confederates had been given a belligerent's rights and therefore must be regarded as a conquered foreign power.

"They are subject to all the liabilities of a vanquished foe," Thaddeus Stevens thundered. "Only Congress may rebuild and readmit the rebellious states to the Union, if they should be judged fit to resume the privileges which they renounced and sought to destroy."

But the Radicals were not in full agreement on the secession issue. Senator Sumner claimed the Southern states had not seceded, as they lacked the constitutional right to do so. By rebelling against the federal government, he believed, they had lost their statehood and reverted again to a territorial status. This meant Congress might prescribe rules and regulations to which "territories" must comply before being granted statehood once more.

Explaining his theory in detail, Sumner said: "This means the rebel states would be treated as outside of their constitutional relations to the Union, and as incapable of restoring themselves to it, except on conditions laid down by Congress."

The debate on the matter often was lofty and pedantic. After all, highly complicated issues were at stake. But sooner or later the controversy reverted to the most perplexing problem of all—the place of the free Negro in American society. Here were no moot questions on constitutional interpretation. Here were human beings, men, women and children, consigned to an inferior place in the American scheme of things for more than two centuries.

Thousands had fought, bled and died to determine whether a black skin must doom a man to a life of slavery that reduced a human being to a chattel, a possession, like a horse or a piece of furniture. It had been decided in fire and agony that slavery no longer had a place in America. But if the "peculiar institution" had been eliminated, what was to become of the former slave?

At the time when the problem was new, when the Negro had just been unfettered and was taking his first uncertain steps to freedom, Americans watched him with wonder and dread. Some held out a hand to help him on his faltering way; others tried to strike him down.

President Andrew Johnson gave no concession to Negro rights beyond stating that ex-slaves were entitled to be "well and humanely governed . . . and to be protected in their . . . person and property."

Beyond this, Johnson would not budge. He told Congress:

I mean to keep this a white man's country. . . . I mean to keep the South in white man's hands. . . . In the progress of nations, Negroes have shown less capacity for government than any other race of people. . . . Whenever left to their own devices they have shown a constant tendency to relapse into barbarism. . . . Of all the dangers which our nation has yet encountered, none are equal to those which must result from the success of the effort . . . to "Africanize" the southern half of our country.

Thaddeus Stevens, wracked with fever and pain, defiantly flung back a reply to the President. His deep-set eyes aflame with anger, Stevens said:

This is *not* a white man's government. To say so . . . violates the fundamental principles of our gospel of liberty. This is *man's* government; the government of *all men* alike.

Senator Henry Wilson of Massachusetts declared:

We must see to it that a man made free . . . is a freeman indeed; that he can go where he pleases, work when and for whom he pleases; that he can sue and be sued; that he can lease and buy and sell and own property, real and personal; that he can go into schools and educate himself and his children . . . and that he walks the earth, proud and erect in the conscious dignity of a free man.

Horace Greeley, the peripatetic editor of the New York *Tribune,* asked for even more. Denouncing state laws that prohibited interracial marriages, Greeley called for their repeal. "Marriage is a personal concern. . . . No law is just which meddles in private lives," he said.

Such demands for racial equality and giving Negroes the vote went beyond anything the average white man, Yank or Rebel, cared to support. The Secretary of Navy, Gideon Welles, wrote:

> I am no advocate for social equality. Nor do I labor for political or civil equality with the Negro. I do not want him at my table, nor do I care to have him in the jury box, or in the legislative hall, or on the bench.

The idealism of the Radicals was mocked and doubted by their foes. The advocates of civil rights for Negroes were lambasted at every turn. According to the Johnsonians, the Radicals were hiding ignoble motives behind a facade of idealism. Enemies of the Radicals found it impossible to believe that any white man could genuinely make equality for Negroes a basis of resistance to Johnson's Reconstruction policies. "Men who think thus are liars, fanatics or insane," a Conservative leader said.

According to the Johnson camp, most Radicals fell under one or more of these descriptions. The line the President's backers took was that the Radicals wanted to raise the Negro only to punish and degrade Southern whites. The cynical Radicals, they said, while pretending to be concerned about the Negro's right to vote, were seeking to win suffrage for him only to capture his vote. In other words, the Radicals cared nothing about Negroes and were using those confused and bewildered people to further their own ends.

One charge made against the Radicals was true. Men such as Stevens, Wade, Chandler and others intended to make the South pay for its "treason." Gideon Welles noted in his diary:

> The Radicals . . . are motivated by hate and revenge. . . . These fanatics want a God to punish, not love, those who do not agree with them.

The desire to make the South "squirm" was not limited to Radical congressmen and senators. Thousands of Northerners, embittered by four years of unrelenting war, yearned for revenge against the Rebels, and the Radicals were their spokesmen.

Thaddeus Stevens echoed the sentiments of many fellow Yankees, in an address to Congress, when he vowed to spend the "small remaining remnant" of his life "punishing traitors."

> A rebellion . . . was waged with fiendish cruelty against the best government on earth [he declaimed]. Did any respectable government ever before allow such high criminals to escape with impunity? They have not been punished as they deserve. They have exchanged forgiveness with the President and been sent on their way rejoicing. . . . I have no sympathy for that morbid sensibility called mercy. . . . I would execute some of the leading rebels. . . . Surely *some* victims must pay for our starved, murdered, slaughtered martyrs.

XII

IF ANY MAN EPITOMIZED the Radicals, it was Thaddeus Stevens. Born with a clubfoot, he endured a miserable childhood; his father, an alcoholic, deserted the family. As a youth, Stevens knew poverty, yet rose to become a wealthy man, the owner of an ironworks at Caledonia, Pennsylvania. When Robert E. Lee invaded that state in July 1863, the Stevens plant was burned to the ground by Confederate troops. Some claim that his venom against Southerners stemmed from this act. Others said he was vengeful because of having been thwarted in his political ambitions. He had failed to win a Senate seat or an appointment to the Cabinet. Still others mentioned a frustrated personal life as the reason. Although Stevens never married, he had a mulatto housekeeper who, gossips whispered, was his mistress. Some put down Stevens' nasty disposition to a chronic arthritis condition which kept him in constant pain.

But these things merely helped shape Stevens into a crusty, acidulous bachelor with a biting wit. Once Lincoln asked his opinion of Simeon Cameron, the Secretary of War, and Stevens tartly replied, "I know Cameron. He is honest. He will not steal a red-hot stove." Pressed by an irate Cameron for an apology, Stevens said, "I am sorry. I misjudged Mr. Cameron. I now withdraw my statement. He *would* steal a red-hot stove."

Stevens, an adroit politician, merely reflected the feelings of numerous rank-and-file Republicans in his virulent anti-Southern speeches. He could point to stacks of letters received from constituents expressing the same sentiments. Most of these letters contained statements such as:

> I resent calling these Southern hounds our Southern brethren. . . . I beg of you to do what you can to have *somebody* convicted and hung and thereby make treason odious.

There were other motives pushing Stevens and the Radicals; revenge played only a small part in their program. Most Republicans—Moderate and Radical—had realistic reasons for wanting to end the Johnson governments in the South and to postpone the seating of Southern congressmen. They were worried that Southern and Western farmers might again unite in the Democratic party. This was the alliance that had controlled national politics for so long in prewar times.

Ironically, if Johnson's Reconstruction had been completed the South would have enjoyed a larger representation in Congress than it had before the war. Before emancipation, only three-fifths of all Negroes had been counted in the apportionment of representatives. Now that they were slaves no longer, *all* Negroes were to be counted, which would give the South a gain of some 15 representatives, who opposed granting voting rights to Negroes.

While the welfare of the Republican party was a primary concern of all party men—Moderate, Conservative and Radical, not all were willing to sell out the ex-slaves and rob them of the chance for first-class citizenship in order to ensure the party's continued success. To some Republicans—mainly Radicals—human needs superceded political needs; they would not abandon the Negro in this critical moment. "If we fail the black man, we fail ourselves," a Radical congressman said. (It was easy to sound noble—Radical political needs, at the moment, involved the Negro.)

Radicals kept up the fight for Negro rights despite the storm of hatred, slander and violence their campaign aroused. Foes of the Radicals resorted to vicious attacks against them. Gideon Welles recorded in his diary that Radical "do-gooders" had only one motive in all their "sanctimonious" speeches and that was to protect the interests of Northern business. According to Welles,

> These Radical patriots are swindling the country while imposing on its credulity. The granting of acts of incorporation, bounties, special privileges, favors, and profligate legislation is shocking.

Much of what Welles said was true. The Thirty-ninth Congress, which repudiated Johnson-inspired governments in the South, was involved with economic legislation. There were discussions on tariff laws to bolster the iron and woolen manufacturers. Proposals for direct or indirect subsidies to commerical interests were enacted; measures benefiting railroad builders were passed. Few requests of Big Business were denied. This was the period of burgeoning capitalism, the sprouting of trusts and monopolies, the era of the oil, rail, coal and iron barons.

The federal government under Republican control gave generous concessions to business; natural resources were turned over to individuals and corporations for private profit. Someone termed the post-Civil War years as the time of the "Big Barbeque," when "Uncle Sam was host to the capitalists and every corporation could gorge itself at the public feeding trough."

Unquestionably, the Radicals were partial to business interests. Stevens was an important Pennsylvania iron manufacturer, a staunch ally of the iron interests in his native state and an associate of the men who ran the Northern Pacific and Pennsylvania Railroads. Senator Zachariah Chandler was a rich Detroit merchant. Congressman Roscoe Conkling, a corporation lawyer, represented New York bankers and railroad interests. Fiery Senator Benjamin Wade was tied in with Western manufacturers and wool growers. Intellectual Senator Charles Sumner ardently supported the textile industries of New England.

That the Radicals closely linked Reconstruction and commerce was no secret. A spokesman for them declared that the Southern congressmen Johnson wanted to seat were striving to "bring about a great reduction in Tariffs, . . . perhaps even institute Free Trade. . . . How sweet and complete will be the revenge of the Rebels if they can ruin the North by Free Trade." Senator Sumner insisted Negro suffrage was necessary to keep out of power the Democrats who would repudiate the public debt and public credit. He asked:

> Are you ready to put your rights, your property and the honor of the nation up for raffle by the betrayers of your country? There is too much at stake . . . to let prejudice against Negroes hold sway.

A feeling was prevalent among certain Radicals that, before the South could be trusted with any significant political power, it must be settled by Northerners, built up by Northern money and indoctrinated with a Northern viewpoint. In short, it was proposed that the former Confederate territory be thoroughly "Northernized"; only then could the South be readmitted to the Union without hesitation or doubts.

In general, Northern businessmen gradually swung over to the Radical side although some of them had supported Johnson at the beginning of his administration. The President's stabs at Reconstruction convinced the capitalists that his policies offered them little, so they promptly switched to the Radicals.

The presence of so many financiers and industrialists in Radical ranks added fuel to anti-Radical charges that the movement was made up of vengeance seekers, crackpots, political opportunists and voracious capitalists. The Johnsonians pointed out that Radicals had ulterior motives and said that the so-called do-gooders were unprincipled men who were using the poor Negro to further their own nefarious purposes.

But whether or not the Radicals were pursuing base and selfish goals, their program was neither evil nor immoral. Most Radicals made idealistic-sounding public statements. If Thaddeus Stevens demanded Negro suffrage in order to punish the South, strengthen the Republican party and preserve the high protective tariff, he also uttered splendid words about the rights to which Negroes were entitled:

> Every man, no matter what his race or color, . . . has an equal right to justice, honesty and fair play with every other man. The law should secure him those rights. The same law which condemns or acquits an African, should condemn or acquit a white man. The same law which gives a verdict in a white man's favor should give a verdict in a black man's favor on the same state of facts. Such is the law of God and should be the law of man.

Similar high-flown sentiments were often expressed by Radical orators on the subject of Negro rights. But their enemies were sceptical and accused them of hypocrisy. One critic railed:

> Your Radical demagogue puts on a false face for the Negro. . . . He cares nothing about the black man, all that matters is to have the blacks on his side. . . . To gain this, the Radical liars will say and do anything.

Perhaps a man such as Thaddeus Stevens really believed that what was good for the Republican party was good for the country; perhaps he would use every available trick to keep the party strong. But no man could justly accuse him of being a hypocrite about the Negro. Most of his adult life had been spent in fighting to obtain social justice for the Negro. (Even in death, according to an unproven story, Stevens demonstrated his feelings about Negroes. According to his wishes, he allegedly was buried in the Negro cemetery of his home town, because segregation was practiced in the white one.)

Nor was Representative George W. Julian of Indiana hypocritical when he said to a Republican audience:

> The real trouble is that *we whites hate the Negro*. . . . It is not his ignorance which offends us, but his color. . . . Let one rule be adopted for black and white, and let us, if possible, dispossess our minds, utterly, of the vile spirit of caste, which brought upon our country all its woes.

Senator Henry Wilson of Massachusetts probably was not deceitful in his speech to white workingmen when he said:

> We Radicals have advocated the rights of the black man, because the black man was the most oppressed type of the toiling men of this country. . . . The man who is the enemy of the *black* laboring man is the enemy of the *white* laboring man the world over. The same influences that go to keep down and crush down the rights of the poor black man bear down and oppress the poor white laboring man.

Although Thaddeus Stevens was rich, prominent and influential, he had fought for free universal schooling and other legislation to benefit the poor people of Pennsylvania. When the war was over, Stevens turned to a different battleground—the struggle for Negro rights, a cause to which he seemed totally committed. The Negroes of Pennsylvania long had known him as a friend. Now the enfeebled old gladiator again entered the lists and flung defiance at his foes. He informed his constituents:

> I care not what you may say of Negro equality. I care not what you say of Radicalism; these are my principles, and with the help of God, I shall die with them.

Stevens was no man to mince words or soften blows. He let everyone, friend or foe, know exactly where he stood. On the subject of Reconstruction, he said:

> I demand a radical reorganization in Southern institutions. . . . This may startle feeble minds and shake weak nerves. So do all great improvements in the political and moral world. It requires a heavy impetus to drive forward a sluggish people. When it was first proposed to free the slaves and arm the blacks, did not half the nation tremble? The prim Conservatives, the snobs, and the male waiting-maids in Congress, were in hysterics.

Before much time had passed, Stevens and his fellow Radicals were to bring on more hysterics in Congress and out with their program of Reconstruction. One thing was certain: No matter how well or how poorly that program fared, something was going to be done for the Negro. As one Radical congressman said:

I pledge that our country shall do something to repay the immense debt we owe the Negroes. I cannot but feel that it was their fervent prayers and strong arms that helped save our Union in the hour of deepest peril.

XIII

THE RADICAL RECONSTRUCTION PLAN was concerned not only with the Negro problem; economics had a major place in the program. The Radical economic policy was founded on measures supporting a high tariff, the national banking system and generous subsidies to railroads. The Radicals felt that these measures would benefit not just a few corporations, groups and individuals, but the nation as a whole.

Giving away public lands, mineral and timber resources to private interests was not regarded with dismay by anyone. In the period immediately following the Civil War, it was universally believed that America's natural resources would last forever and that it was better to put them to productive use under private sponsorship than let vast areas remain idle.

In a society of free farmers and expanding industries, it was assumed that every man had an equal chance to become rich. The desire for material success became a national mania. Stevens advised his fellow Americans, "of all creeds, colors and origins," to push out into the West, "where there was land and untold riches locked in the earth." He urged that manufacturing and industry be enabled to grow.

To Stevens the new railroads, factories, foundries and shops, and the spreading industries of the North were part of American progress toward a fuller and richer life for all. On the other hand, he saw the Southern plantation system as a world "of sloth, backwardness and feudal darkness."

According to the Radicals, America stood at the crossroads; either it followed the road of progress with its bright future, or else it turned back along the path of the prewar days with human bondage and outmoded methods. Surely the war had not been fought and so many lives sacrificed to keep the country at a standstill. The South had been defeated in the name of humanity and progress. But President Johnson's Reconstruction threatened to rob the North of its hard-won victory.

Fear existed in the North that Southerners were plotting a new rebellion and the war would have to be fought again in five, ten or 20 years. This dread was largely responsible for much of the postwar Yankee attitudes toward the South. The Northerners wanted security for the future and indemnity for the past; they wanted to be sure that the South never again would be in a position to take up arms against them.

This suspicion of Southern motives undoubtedly gained much support in the North for Radical Reconstruction. The astute Frenchman, Georges Clemenceau, then a working newsman, summing up the American postwar scene, wrote:

> When anyone has for four successive years joined in such a struggle as that which the United States has seen . . . he desires not to lose the dearly bought fruits of so many painful sacrifices. When the war ended, the North was concerned not to let itself be tricked out of what it had spent so much trouble and perseverance to win.

Possibly the greatest mistake President Johnson had made was to assume that the South could run its domestic affairs along lines that marked a complete break with the past. To do this required leaders far more capable and clearheaded than any the South had. Where men of discretion and restraint were wanted, only rabble-rousing incompetents could be found.

With incomprehensible arrogance, Southern postwar leaders defied the Yankees at every turn. Northern demands for decent treatment of former slaves were answered with bloody race riots in Memphis and New Orleans and by the infamous Black Codes. Instead of breaking with their recent past, the Southerners elected blatant Rebels to office, thus making a mockery of the Johnson-inspired state governments.

Both Southern defiance and Yankee vindictiveness stirred Radical opposition to Johnson. From its opening session in December 1865, the Thirty-ninth Congress was pitted against the President's program and took steps to overthrow it. The first act of resistance by Congress was the refusal to seat in House or Senate the men elected by the 11 former Confederate states. This halted swift congressional recognition of the Johnson-approved state governments. (In February 1866, the ruling bloc of Moderate and Radical Republicans agreed that no congressman from any Southern state should be seated in either house until both houses had cleared the state to have such representation.)

Another move by Congress was to set up the Joint Committee on Reconstruction, which was to investigate conditions in the South, receive all bills and resolutions connected with Reconstruction, and make recommendations to Congress for future legislation on the subject. The Joint Committee met almost daily for several months, probing every aspect of conditions in the South. After an intensive investigation, the Joint Committee delivered its report to Congress on April 28, 1866.

According to the Committee, when the war ended the Confederate states had been "wholly disorganized and without proper civil government. . . . Anarchy reigned." It was recommended that not only should elections held under such circumstances be invalidated, but these states also should be refused representation in Congress until full civil rights were extended to *all* the people, and former rebel leaders were removed from office.

Furthermore, continued the report, which contained volumes of testimony from people living in the South, the recent rebellion had been put down under the guidance of the legislative, executive and judicial branches of the government, and not by the President alone. Hence, President Johnson was not empowered to set terms deciding how the South might return to the Union. It was decided that, as the majority of Southerners still retained bitter hostility for the federal government, they should be barred from any voice in Washington until further notice.

It soon became apparent that Congress meant to treat the South with severity despite President Johnson's wishes. The Chief Executive unwisely had worsened his own position with Congress by vetoing two bills aimed at protecting Southern Negroes which Moderate Republicans felt he should have signed. The first was a measure to extend the life and increase the powers of the Freedmen's Bureau, a wartime agency that had been created to help Negroes. The second one was a Civil Rights Bill "to protect all persons in the United States in their civil rights."

Johnson's advisors had urged him to sign both bills even if he did not agree with them. They realized he would speed up a split with Congress should he veto the bills. In addition, spokesmen for the Moderate bloc had warned the President that passage of the two bills was their minimum condition for continuing to support the administration.

However, Johnson vetoed both the Freedmen's Bureau Bill and the Civil Rights Bill. He had turned thumbs down on the Freedmen's Bureau because an agency "for the support of indigent persons in the United States was never contemplated by the authors of the Constitution."

In rejecting the Civil Rights Bill, he argued:

> This bill provides the Negro with safeguards which
> go infinitely beyond any that the Federal Government

has ever provided for the white race. In fact the distinction of race and color is by the bill made to operate in favor of the colored and against the white race.

Johnson had justification in vetoing these bills. It was possible that the Supreme Court would find them an unconstitutional infringement of States' Rights. It was to safeguard the Civil Rights Bill that the Radicals demanded the Fourteenth Amendment. They also feared an adverse Supreme Court decision.

Congress rose in almost united anger against Johnson. On April 9, 1866, the Civil Rights Bill was passed in spite of the President and on July 16, 1866, his veto of the Freedmen's Bureau Bill was overridden.

President Johnson seemed determined to carry forward his vendetta with Congress. Instead of trying to smooth out the differences he had with that body, the Chief Executive aggravated the grievances by his intemperate attitude toward the legislators. But, by sticking to his principles, Johnson had no alternative.

On February 22, 1866, just after he had vetoed the Freedmen's Bureau Bill, Johnson made an impromptu speech to a Washington's Birthday crowd gathered outside the White House. He aimed a vituperative attack at Congress. Hinting darkly that the Radicals wanted dictatorial powers, he warned his listeners that "certain interests" were plotting his assassination.

> I stand before you unafraid [the President cried]. I fought traitors and treason in the South. . . . Now when I turn around, and at the other end of the line find men . . . who will stand opposed to the restoration of the

Union of these States, I am free to say to you that I am still in their field . . . ready to battle traitors North or South.

Pressed by the audience to name the men he believed were traitors, Johnson answered:

You ask me who they are? I say Thaddeus Stevens of Pennsylvania is one; I say Mr. Sumner of the Senate is another; and Wendell Phillips is another. . . . And these are not the only ones.

The President ignored all advice to temper his remarks and try to patch up things with his congressional foes. But Johnson raged out of control. During the congressional elections of 1866, he stumped for candidates of his choice. The campaign tour took him as far west as Chicago and St. Louis. Wherever he stopped the President spoke, convinced that the people would back him and his Reconstruction policies.

Possibly Johnson could have swung public opinion to his side had he chosen his words carefully and conducted himself in a dignified manner. Instead, the President campaigned "like a wild man," according to one observer. He delivered speeches described by Gideon Welles as "rambling, vulgar, vindictive and loaded with self-pity." Rather than helping his cause, Johnson did it irreparable damage. Even his most ardent supporter, Congressman Henry J. Raymond of New York, editor of *The New York Times,* noted in that paper:

I believe the country has never seen so melancholy a spectacle as Mr. Johnson . . . during this current cam-

paign. . . . It is mortifying to watch . . . the President
cast aside all dignity and thus sully his exalted office.

Apparently, Johnson had lost all restraint and was re-
verting to the rough-and-tumble tactics of the old days in
Tennessee where insult, mudslinging and slander were
accepted political weapons. However suitable such tactics might have been on the frontier, they had no place
on the national level, especially when employed by the
President of the United States. Even at that early stage of
his administration (summer and fall 1866) certain Radicals in Congress began speaking about instituting impeachment proceedings against the President.

During the 1866 congressional elections, about the
only solid support Johnson received was from his former
colleagues in the Democratic party. He could not fully
have relished such support because the Democrats relied
upon appeals to the racial prejudices of Northern voters.
They conducted a vicious campaign filled with racist slo-
gans to stoke anti-Negro sentiments. Democratic speakers warned:

> The Radicals want to push the "niggers" into your par-
> lors and bedrooms! Down with the "nigger" party! Up
> with the White Man's Party!

According to the Democrats, the Radicals (read "Republicans") planned to make the South "a black man's
paradise." Not only that, they were going to "turn white
workingmen out of their jobs and fill the shops with
cheap 'nigger' labor." Frank Blair, chief of the Johnson
forces in Missouri, declared that the "announced policy"

of the Radicals was to form a regular army of "black mercenaries" who would "keep down the white man with a ring of bayonets."

The Republicans, of all political hues and shadings, ran a campaign no less vituperative than that of the Johnson camp. They hurled every imaginable sort of charge against the President. He drank too much; he had helped plot Lincoln's assassination; he was conspiring to turn over the government to copperheads and rebels.

It was at this time that the Republicans uncorked a style of speechmaking which became known as "waving the bloody shirt." This was a rabble-rousing technique aimed at keeping aflame wartime partisan passions, matching in kind the racist rantings of the Democrats. It's main purpose was to link the Democrats with treason, the Republicans with all things patriotic. A typical "bloody shirt" speech was one delivered by Oliver P. Morton, Indiana's Civil War governor, who said in part:

> Every unregenerate rebel, . . . every deserter, every sneak who ran away from the draft calls himself a Democrat. . . . Every wolf in sheep's clothing who pretends to preach the gospel but proclaims the righteousness of man-selling and slavery; everyone who shoots down Negroes in the streets, burns up Negro schoolhouses and meeting houses, and murders women and children by the light of their own flaming dwellings calls himself a Democrat. . . . In short, the Democratic party may be described as a common sewer and loathsome receptacle, into which is emptied every element of treason North and South, every element of inhumanity and barbarism which has dishonored the age.

The elections ended in overwhelming defeat for Johnson and his policies. Despite the beclouded issues and undisciplined conduct of the campaign, the voters heeded the Republican warning that the Democrats, through President Johnson's Reconstruction program, would lose the peace for the North, restore leading rebels to power, reestablish slavery and pave the way for another Civil War. These dire threats won for the Republicans a landslide victory; they gained control of every state legislature in the North, won every Northern governorship and captured more than two-thirds majorities in both houses of Congress.

XIV

By ROUTING the Democrats and the Johnson forces, the Radical Republicans, who now held sway in Washington, found themselves in an unenviable position. After belaboring the President's Reconstruction plans, they had to come up with a better one, or else be confronted by the ire of an outraged public.

The Radicals could easily override his vetoes to legislation but, as Chief Executive, Johnson had to enforce the laws once they were passed. He was therefore in a position to sabotage Radical enactments by laxity in carrying them out; no one doubted that would be precisely what the President was going to do.

President Johnson, although repudiated by the voters, was not the least of the Radicals' difficulties. Radical power depended on a continued unity with the Moderate faction; it was anybody's guess how long this marriage of political convenience would last. Cynics gave it a few months. "Once the Moderates get over being so mad at Johnson, they'll start scrapping with the Radicals; those birds never belonged in the same flock," a Washington newspaperman said.

The strength of the old ruling class in the South also presented an obstacle to the Radicals. The landed aristocracy and former slaveowners, though defeated in war, still retained amazing prestige and power among the people. Instead of turning against those who had led the disastrous conflict, Southerners were welded more closely to them by the searing flames of the debacle they had endured jointly.

It became clear to the Radicals that the only group in the South uncommitted to the old order was the 4,000,000 ex-slaves. No Radical program had a chance of success without widespread Negro support.

Thus, the Negro again became the center of a controversy not of his own making. As a slave he had been victimized; now, as a freeman he was still the victim, trapped between powerful forces, caught in the quicksands of politics.

By 1866, few of the former slaves still had any link with their African past or ancestral cultures. For more than two hundred years they had been born, lived, toiled and died on American soil. Denied citizenship, or even basic human rights, the Negro yearned to become a full-fledged member of the white man's community for which he had shed blood and tears, for which he had given his sweat and muscle. Black men had built roads, plowed fields, dammed rivers, cut forests, erected homes—all for the white man. He had been paid by lash and rope, by being held in bondage, by exclusion from the mainstream of American society.

After more than two centuries of servitude most Southerners thought the Negro should have been content to remain servile. But many Negroes knew there was something better. He cherished a dream of freedom, although he had no concept of what freedom entailed. To most slaves it meant a strip of land—"forty acres and a mule" —and the dignity of having one's own place in the sun.

Most slaves were illiterate. In prewar days it had been illegal to teach Negro bondsmen to read and write. When the war was over, the Negro had been thrust out into the world to fend for himself; by the stroke of a pen in far-off Washington, he was declared free.

But he was unprepared for his new responsibilities. The former slaves knew how to earn a living as freemen; they were skilled blacksmiths, carpenters, cooks, bakers, mechanics; they were farmers, fieldhands, coachmen and butlers. What they lacked was the opportunity for employment as free workers.

Yet, even if the barriers which excluded Negroes from most jobs had not existed, the newly freed bondsmen suffered from crippling handicaps. The very nature of slavery destroyed a man's initiative and ability to think independently. In all his life a slave seldom had to rely upon himself; he was told what to do and when to do it. Slaveowners demanded docility and servility; any Negro who behaved otherwise was subjected to swift punishment. The very fact that he was a slave, that he was nothing more than his master's personal property, made the Negro feel inferior to the white man.

He came to freedom "broken in spirit and with the long, long habit of servility," declared *Harper's Weekly* in advising friends of the Negro that a great deal must not be expected from him. And the article continued:

> They have so much to unlearn. . . . It will take a very long time before the browbeaten slave can overcome his fear and suspicion of the whites who enchained him.

Freedom came like a thunderbolt. The shackles were loosened, the fetters broken. Southern slaveholders had boasted, as did one Georgia planter:

> My blacks won't budge from my land. . . . Why, it's been a Garden of Eden for them. . . . I've never mistreated a slave in my life. . . . I handle them as I do a good horse or a hunting dog,—with kindness most of the time, with firmness when necessary.

But to their chagrin, the first thing most ex-slaves did was to quit the "Garden of Eden" in which they had labored.

The Negroes took to the road after discovering they could roam at will. There were many reasons for this wanderlust. Some wanted "to see what was on the other side of the hill." Some went looking for husbands, wives, children, friends and relatives from whom they had been separated during the time of slavery. Others wandered into cities and towns seeking work, schooling, help. It was a mass exodus of the oppressed from the scenes of oppression.

The more intelligent and spirited recent slaves went

off with fixed purposes; the majority, merely for the sake of being footloose. A great number of them suffered from want and privation as they roved aimlessly from place to place. The Southern whites treated them inhospitably, often with hostility. They watched resentfully the course of this vast upheaval, a reaction which was not unexpected.

The course of freedom was not a smooth one. The only friends the Negroes had were the Radicals in Washington; and those far-off white men did what they could when it benefited *them*. Legislative machinery moved ponderously but the times called for speedy action. However, for whatever their reasons, the Radicals tried.

The first step was to do away with the repressive and obnoxious Black Codes; these odious regulations were unsuitable as rules for freemen of any color. They erected "prisons without bars" for the Negroes. The Radicals attempted to create a new atmosphere in the South, one in which Negroes would have the same political, legal and economic rights as the whites enjoyed.

It was recognized by some Radicals that there could be no political and legal equality for the freedmen unless they were given economic aid as well—at least in the formative stages of the so-called New South. Four million persons had been released from bondage, cast out into the world with nothing, trained only to be slaves. They had no funds, no tools, no property; they were set free without shelter, homeless, rootless, owning not even the clothing they wore. Neither Lincoln's Emancipation Proclamation nor the Thirteenth Amendment contained provisions forcing slaveowners to compensate their bondsmen for past labor, nor did the federal government offer them any financial aid.

The articlulate ex-slave Frederick Douglass, long a spokesman for his people, vividly stated their case:

> The freedmen . . . were sent away empty-handed, without money, without friends and without a foot of land to stand upon. Old and young, sick and well, they were turned loose to the open sky, naked to their enemies.

It was this economic deprivation and helplessness of the slaves which the Radicals recognized as the gravest danger that faced them. Unable to cope in a competitive society, entrapped by the vicious Black Codes, the Negroes were free in name only.

The threat of a return to bondage of a different sort was real and constant. Unless the Negroes could win economic independence, landholders could menace them with a terrible weapon. Under the vagrancy clauses of the Black Codes, they could be forced into a "slavery" almost as onerous as the one they just had escaped.

The Joint Committee on Reconstruction gathered ample evidence to ascertain this peril. It soon became obvious that winning civil and political rights for the Negro had no meaning unless he also could be guaranteed economic stability. The facts uncovered by the Committee merely underlined added difficulties to an old problem. Even before the war ended, economic deprivation among freed Negroes had reached epidemic proportions in areas of the South penetrated by Union troops. Wherever the Yankees came, Negroes flocked to them. General William T. Sherman was overwhelmed by "swarms of blacks" as he pushed from Atlanta to Savannah on his historic march. The situation worsened in Savannah; a host of runaway Negroes—men, women and children—descended upon Sherman. He had difficulty feeding the hordes of hungry people who had converged trustfully on the conquering Yankees, the bringers of freedom.

The naïve slaves gave no thought to the lack of work, poverty, want and hunger that faced them. "Massa Linkum's" soldiers had come, a-bringin' the Jubilee, Glory Hallelujah! What to do with freedom never had occurred to these simple souls. The Day of Jubilee was at hand, a day to be greeted with song, with tears and with laughter. Forever free; slaves no more! Only that had meaning to them.

But after weeks of near starvation, of suffering and misery, the Negroes finally realized that freedom was not heaven on earth. With it came problems none of them ever before had faced. As slaves, Master had taken care of their physical needs; Master had supplied food, clothing and shelter. Master had looked after his slaves the way a shepherd tends his flock.

But the Negroes were men, not animals. They asked more of life than grits, a pair of overalls and a shanty which kept out neither heat, cold nor rain. Nor did they want to remain chattels, to be bought and sold, available to the highest bidder. The Negroes began to see them-

selves as grown people, not children; they longed for
schooling and the chance to rise from their lowly place.
Now that they had freedom, it must not be wasted.

Early in 1865, Secretary of War Edwin M. Stanton
had paid a visit to General Sherman at Savannah. The
General and Stanton, both deeply concerned over the
conditions existing among the freedmen hanging on the
fringes of the army, called a meeting of 20 Negro leaders
and asked what could be done to better the lot of the ex-
slaves.

The reply came quickly:

> Land, . . . if we had land, we'd be able to look after
> ourselves. . . . We'd work the land, plow it and seed
> it, make it bloom. . . . Give us land.

It was a sound solution. Most Negroes knew how to
farm. For them the vision of freedom included a plot of
good earth—"forty acres and a mule." With his own land
a man was equal to anyone; land made the difference;
the soil didn't care if the plowman's skin was black or
white.

Perhaps a broad land-reform program in the South, involving a revolutionary breakup of the great plantations,
might have changed the course of American history.
Such a move had been recommended as early as 1864,
when a commission had been sent South by the government to examine the condition of Negroes and offer suggestions for bettering it. The commission had declared:

> No such thing as a free, democratic society can exist
> in any country where all lands are owned by one class

of men and cultivated by another. . . . Under such circumstances, a system of serfdom develops.

These were strange words to describe the situation in a country which had been founded on principles of democracy, liberty and equality. Especially when, in 1863, the world's most despotic country, Tsarist Russia, had put into effect a land-reform policy that released the downtrodden Russian peasant, the *muzhik*, from the oppressive serfdom under which he had existed for centuries.

XV

GENERAL WILLIAM TECUMSEH SHERMAN was no re-former, no abolitionist, no Radical. "Cump" Sherman was a hard-bitten soldier, a realist unafraid to face cold facts. In 1865, "Uncle Billy," as his men had nicknamed him, decided to do something about the destitution of the Negroes. He took a bold step to help them by a large-scale redistribution of land in one region of the Deep South that had fallen under his control.

Special Field Order Number 15, signed by Sherman, set aside the South Carolina and Georgia sea islands south of Charleston, and the abandoned rice paddies along the rivers, for a distance of some 30 miles inland, as Negro settlements. This wide stretch was broken up into tracts of 40 acres each to which Negro farmers were given temporary title, until such time as Congress de-cided on a final disposition.

The program was directed by General Rufus Saxton, who had genuine feeling and concern for the former slaves. Given the title Inspector of Settlements and Plantations, Saxton placed some 40,000 Negroes on these lands. He was able to show the Committee on Reconstruction that the program was a smashing success.

Despite the effectiveness of the sea-island experiment, President Johnson opposed it and, in January 1866, removed General Saxton from his post as project director. Eventually all the confiscated lands were returned to their original owners. (The eviction of the Negroes was accompanied by violence. The ex-slaves resisted and numerous clashes took place.)

A similar, but smaller land redistribution took place some 25 miles south of Vicksburg, in an area known as Davis Bend. In 1864, six plantations, including those owned by Jefferson Davis and his brother, Joseph, were seized by U.S. officials.

Some 75 Negro farmers were settled there. They worked so well that each man gleaned a profit of $1,000 after expenses. The next year the confiscated land was divided into 40-acre sections among the Negroes, who farmed cooperatively and harvested more than $150,000 net profit.

Writing of this project, a historian said, "A wiser and more benevolent government might well have seen in Davis Bend the suggestion of a long-time program for making the Negro a self-reliant, prosperous and enterprising element of the population." However, President Johnson pardoned the owners of the Davis Bend plantations, except the Davis brothers, and returned the land to them. Once again, Negro tenants were evicted by force.

Congress furiously debated land reform through confiscation. Arguing that confiscation was a "logical part of emancipation," Senator Charles Sumner declared that the plantations, which he labeled "so many nurseries of Rebellion," had to be broken up "and the freedmen must have the pieces."

Confiscation's most fiery advocate was the ailing warrior, Thaddeus Stevens. In a speech on the subject, he remarked:

> When that wise man, the Emperor of Russia, set free twenty-two million serfs, he compelled their masters to give them homesteads upon the very soil which they had tilled. . . . He said, in noble words, "They have earned this, they have worked upon the land for ages, and they are entitled to it."

The United States, according to Stevens, could do no less for its freed slaves. He stated:

> The whole fabric of Southern society *must* be changed, and never can it be done if this opportunity is lost. How can republican institutions, free schools, free churches . . . exist in a mingled community of nabobs and serfs? If the South is ever to be made a safe Republic let her lands be cultivated by the toil of the owners, or the free labor of intelligent citizens. This must be done though it drive her Nobility into exile.

Stevens outlined a concrete procedure for confiscation. He proposed that it be applied to some 70,000 of the "chief rebels" who owned about 394,000,000 acres of land. Thus, only about five percent of the whites living in the South would be affected. To dispose of the seized land, Stevens suggested that each adult freedman be given no more than 40 acres and supplied with farming implements and a mule. The remaining land should be sold to help defray the costs of the war, provide pension funds for disabled veterans and compensate loyal Southerners who had suffered property damages during the war.

When a colleague told Stevens that his plan was inhuman, that it would ruin 70,000 Southern landholders, the caustic Pennsylvanian said:

> Pray tell me, sir, is it not far easier and more beneficial to exile 70,000 bloated, proud and defiant rebels, than to ship out of the country 4,000,000 Negro laborers, native to the soil and loyal to the government? Yet, I heard you raise no objection when the late President purposed to do precisely that.

Despite the support of Stevens, Sumner, Julian and other Radicals, Congress rejected confiscation specifically and land reform generally. The reason was that many Radicals failed to grasp the need for rendering the Negro economic aid. They chose to believe that laws and constitutional amendments granting him civil rights, the ballot and freedom were sufficient to set the Negro on the road to equality. Cloaking themselves in righteous idealism, the legislators refused to concede that laws, in order to be effective, had to be enforced. If Radicals did not fully understand the issue, then it can be understood why Johnson and the Moderates did not see it.

With ex-slaves completely dependent on their former masters for employment, even the best laws, like good intentions, accomplished nothing. Legislation to uplift economically dependent people who were subjected to extreme racial prejudice would never be carried out.

The continuing deprivation of the Negro convinced Southerners that the "nigger" was inherently inferior. It lent weight to the racist theory that granting Negroes even the slightest political leeway would be disaster. How could a passel of shiftless "niggers" fit into decent, law-abiding communities? Southern racists—and Northern ones as well—revived all the stale descriptions of Negroes. They were a stupid, worthless, irresponsible, childish, superstitious lot, fit for nothing better than the most menial tasks. John Van Buren, a son of the eighth President of the United States, spoke the language of rabid Southern racism when he sneered, "Your 'nigger' is chiefly fit to black boots and cut hair."

This vicious caricature of Negro capabilities still prevailed, although the former slaves had shown themselves to be fully able to perform almost any job well when given a fair chance.

The failure of his friends to appreciate the importance for him to have economic stability and economic independence eventually drove the Negro to the bottom of the social order. It would take him decades of struggle and bloodshed to climb out.

Not only Congressmen lacked the vision to see this. One of the best allies the American Negro ever had, William Lloyd Garrison, a dedicated abolitionist leader, also made the same blunder. After the Thirteenth Amendment was adopted, Garrison decided to dissolve the militant American Anti-Slavery Society. Garrison felt the Negro no longer needed assistance; the fight for the Negro had ended triumphantly with the downfall of slavery.

Just as crusaders had done before and since, Garrison cared only about his own cause. It did not concern him that freedom brought the Negro added problems, among them that of earning of living. But Garrison saw no great principles at stake in the grinding, mundane day-by-day struggle for subsistence. Now that the Negro was free, Garrison decided, he might take his place in society and enjoy all its benefits. This was idealistic, but unrealistic thinking.

Garrison, so conscious of the Negro's plight as a slave, seemed to forget that nothing had changed once the shackles of bondage were removed. The Negro still had a handicap—his skin was black. Only because of this, he had been enslaved; only this physiological accident had set him apart from his fellowman. That same black skin now hampered the free Negro in his "pursuit of happiness." To the prejudiced white man, he remained a lowly slave. Not until the Negro could stand on his own feet, without economic restraint, could he truly be a free American.

Massive and constructive land reform in the South might have blazed the trail to full Negro emancipation on every level. But it did not materialize. Most Congressmen were against tampering with private-property rights. Land could be secured for Negroes only by confiscation, along lines such as those laid down by Stevens. But only a few Washington lawmakers had any taste for taking another man's land (even that of a rebel) and parceling it out to someone else. This smacked too much of social revolution!

The only legislators favoring confiscation were Radical zealots. They could rally only scant support for a course of action which the majority of their colleagues (and the public as a whole) feared would shake the American social structure to its very foundations.

Another highly influential group also opposed land reform and redistribution through confiscation. Northern capitalists and businessmen, Yankees who had purchased Southern cotton plantations or invested in the building of factories down South, fought hard to prevent any land seizures to benefit the Negro. They needed him to chop their cotton and to work in their factories.

Should the Negro get "forty acres and a mule," he would be on his own and lost to the labor market. Without property, without worldly goods, the former slaves were an endless source of cheap factory labor—North and South.

Also Negro workers were a weapon the capitalists could use to throttle the growing movement among white workers toward trade unionism. They presented a threat to prevent strikes. Trade unionists, who downed tools to win better working conditions and higher wages, could be replaced by black men at less pay. Freed slaves must not be given independence, not when they were likely candidates for what had become known as "industrial slavery" in the shops and factories.

However, the Radical Republicans were not totally

blind to the fact that the Negroes and the poor whites were suffering, because of the war-wrought dislocation of the plantation system. Private charities obviously could not cope with all the destitution spread throughout the former Confederacy. Federal intervention was needed.

In March 1865, Congress had created the Bureau of Refugees, Freedmen, and Abandoned Lands under the War Department. The sonorous title soon was shortened to the Freedmen's Bureau. Its function was to supply food, clothing and medical care for both poverty-stricken white refugees and freed Negro slaves. In addition, the Bureau was to provide general help for freedmen, work, schooling and financial assistance to tide them over during their transition from slavery to freedom. Bureau field offices were centers of advice, guidance and leadership for uprooted, confused former slaves. A helping hand also was extended to any white man seeking assistance.

Under this act, the Bureau was to close shop a year after the war ended. As that anniversary approached, it became increasingly clear that the Bureau had not overcome the complex social problems plaguing the South. Its life had to be extended, its powers broadened. The Committee on Reconstruction obtained evidence to back this. Testimony given before the Committee revealed shocking mistreatment of free Negroes. Under the Black Codes, landlords hired them to work in the fields at starvation wages and sometimes refused to pay them after the job was finished. In the Deep South, Negroes who protested were beaten, and even murdered, by bands of white vigilantes specifically organized for the purpose of oppressing freedmen.

These and other abuses indicated that the work of the Freedmen's Bureau had by no means been concluded. Accordingly, Congress, on February 19, 1866, passed a new Freedmen's Bureau Bill. The enactment indefinitely extended the agency's life and empowered it to supervise not only labor contracts involving Negroes, but also to try by special courts anyone charged with depriving freedmen of their civil rights.

President Johnson promptly vetoed the bill, claiming that it was unnecessary, violated the Constitution and impinged on states' rights. Congress repassed it over the veto and the bill became law on July 16, 1866.

Directed by one-armed General Oliver O. Howard, the Freedmen's Bureau was run forcefully and efficiently. However, both General Howard and the Bureau were subjected to sharp criticism from white Southerners and their Northern sympathizers. Because the Bureau functioned so well, critics bitterly complained that its agents were fomenting discontent among the Negroes.

It was charged that Bureau administrators "filled the blacks with all sorts of lying promises." Graft and corruption were widespread, according to the enemies of the Bureau. But the main gripe against the agency was that it meddled in matters which were no concern of the federal government. "The blacks are our affair," a Southern leader grumbled. He went on:

> We don't like blue-nosed Yankees poking around, stir-
> ring up the "niggers"; spoiling them with money; teach-

ing them to sass us. The Bureau people are setting the stage for trouble—big trouble.

Any agency, whether run privately or operated by the government, that had been established to help Negroes attain full citizenship would have stirred Southern antagonism. Racists wanted Negroes to stand hat in hand, stammering, shuffling, servile, in the presence of whites. Any shift in Negro attitudes roused Southern resentment. Those encouraging change became targets of racist wrath.

Undoubtedly, some charges about the Freedmen's Bureau were true. Some Bureau agents stole or misappropriated funds; some spread discontent among the slaves by dangling unattainable goals before them. (Ironically, Bureau agents sometimes mistreated Negroes under their jurisdiction. In Mississippi, an agent acted as a one-man kangaroo court for the planters, punishing former slaves in his district who violated the Black Codes.)

Partisan writers have attacked the Bureau as an organization of fanatical do-gooders who pandered to the whims of Negroes and gave the whites a hard time. But such charges, as well as accusations of widespread corruption within the Bureau, went largely unproved.

President Johnson, openly hostile to the Bureau's activities, searched for evidence against it. In 1866, he sent General Joseph S. Fullerton and General James B. Steedman to investigate every aspect of the Freedmen's Bureau.

Since both Steedman and Fullerton shared Johnson's feelings about the agency, they intended to dig up anything they could to blacken it. In North Carolina, the generals did come across a Bureau scandal; but this gave them small comfort as it involved mistreatment of Negroes, not whites. The investigation proved such a failure that Johnson called off the Southern tour of his generals and abruptly terminated their mission.

During its years of life (the Freedmen's Bureau lasted only until 1869) the agency made a decent record of constructive achievement. Not only did the Bureau look after thousands of indigent ex-slaves, but also, under its guidance, the first schools for Negroes in the Southern states were established (including Howard University, in 1867).

A shortage of funds hampered extension of educational facilities, but with the cooperation of private benevolent societies, inroads were made to wipe out illiteracy among Negroes. The Bureau protected Negroes from the Black Codes by setting conditions of labor and supervising the drawing up of labor contracts. In most areas, the Freedmen's Bureau was the only defender of Negro civil rights.

But after three years, Congress dropped the Bureau, a social experiment without precedent in America. Only Congressmen dedicated to the Negro cause continued to support further appropriations for such a controversial project. Few knights in shining armor held seats on Capitol Hill. Public opinion in the North, molded by the newspapers, ran against the Freedmen's Bureau. Yellow journalists worked overtime to smear the Bureau. Editorials and cartoons lambasted it. It was easier for the people to believe sensational stories about corruption, bumbling and misuse of funds, than not. Bombarded by letters from constituents demanding an end to the Bureau, Congressmen knuckled under. To mollify the irate voters, they put an end to the agency.

Liquidation of the Freedmen's Bureau left the pressing problems of the Negroes unresolved. But the federal government once again stepped in, this time not to alleviate the economic difficulties of the ex-slaves, but to protect their civil and political rights.

XVI

CONSCIOUS OF NEED for legislation to safeguard civil
liberties of former slaves, Congress had passed the Civil
Rights Act of April 9, 1866 the same year that Congress
had passed the Freedmen's Bureau Act. This bill stated
that "all persons born in the United States and not subject to any foreign power, excluding Indians," were to be
considered citizens of the United States. This clarified
the status of Negroes, who had been adjudged not to be
citizens by the U. S. Supreme Court in the Dred Scott
Case decision of 1857.

Besides defining U.S. citizenship, the Act also provided that citizens "of every race and color" were to enjoy "full and equal benefits of all laws and proceedings
for the security of person and property." Also, all citizens
were to be subject "to like punishment, pains and
penalties and to none other."

Convicted violators of the law might be given fines,
imprisonment or both; the federal courts were armed
with sufficient powers to enforce the act.

No sooner had Congress sent him the Bill than Johnson vetoed the measure; it was promptly passed over his veto. Then, because Radicals and Moderates feared that the Supreme Court would declare the Civil Rights Acts unconstitutional, its important clauses were incorporated into the Fourteenth Amendment.

This Amendment, ratified July 28, 1868, stated:

> All persons born or naturalized within the United States, and subject to the jurisdiction thereof, are citizens of the United States and of the State wherein they reside.

The Amendment prohibited states from enacting laws "which shall abridge the privileges or immunities of citizens of the United States." No state might "deprive any person of life, liberty or property without due process of law." Nor could any state "deny to any person within its jurisdiction the equal protection of the laws." As originally stated, the Amendment read: "Congress shall have the power . . ." but this was modified by giving power to the states.

(After the Reconstruction period, the Fourteenth Amendment was seldom applied when the civil rights of Negroes were infringed, but federal courts rigorously enforced it when any state tried to regulate railroads or other corporations.)

Some historians have claimed that the Radicals who shaped the Fourteenth Amendment were more interested in protecting corporations than Negroes. (The courts used the Amendment to set aside regulatory legislation against corporations as violations of the "due process" clause.) Perhaps an economic and not a social basis for writing the Fourteenth Amendment did exist; at the time, corporations were besieging friends in Congress to protect them against state and local laws. One of those who wrote the Amendment alleged that he had phrased the "due process" clause "word for word and syllable for syllable" to protect the rights of Big Business.

Whether or not this was so, Thaddeus Stevens, speaking on the Amendment in Congress, revealed motivation of another sort among its sponsors:

> The proposed enactment will serve to correct the unjust legislation of the states . . . such as the Black Codes . . . so . . . that the law which operates upon one man will operate equally on all. . . . Whatever law punishes a white man . . . shall punish the black man precisely in the same way and to the same degree. . . . Whatever law allows the white man to testify in court shall allow the man of color to do the same.

In that era, neither Negroes nor the Radicals thought of social segregation as the most burning issue. They believed civil, political and economic rights were of far greater moment. Occasionally a Negro leader talked against segregation; once in a while, a Radical such as Sumner protested the practice. At best, the traditional relationships between the races were challenged only sporadically. Integration was beyond the thinking of that day. Even schools supported by the Freedmen's Bureau were segregated. The Bureau's most enlightened workers never pressed for the intermingling of Negro and white children at the font of learning.

Neither the majority of Congressmen who backed the Fourteenth Amendment nor the states which ratified it intended to disturb long-established local racial customs. A few Radical idealists, Senator Charles Sumner in particular, tried to do away with segregation by law. Sumner introduced legislation which would have obliged Southern states to establish "public schools open to all without distinction of race and color."

Further, he urged the Senate to appropriate federal subsidies for biracial public schools and to pass a Civil Rights Act which would outlaw all forms of segregation as violations of the Fourteenth Amendment. He was repeatedly voted down, but he continued his losing fight until he died in 1874.

Segregationists, North and South, battled Sumner all along the line. Their objections to integration were still being echoed in the 1950s and 1960s. They claimed separation of the races did not violate civil rights and that the Fourteenth Amendment was never intended to interfere with purely social matters. The segregationists also warned that attempts to integrate public schools would destroy the school system itself. To this, Sumner countered that segregated schools were "an ill disguised violation of the principle of equality." He contended that segregation harmed both Negro and white children.

It was not until 1875, a year after Sumner's death, that Congress, provoked into action by the excesses being committed against Negroes in the South, finally passed the Civil Rights Act of 1875, which declared in its preamble:

It is essential to just government that we recognize the
equality of all men before the law, and . . . it is the
duty of government in its dealings with people to mete
out equal and exact justice to all, of whatever nativity,
race, color, or persuasion, religious and political.

Under the Act, all persons regardless of color or race,
were guaranteed "the full and equal enjoyment of the ac-
commodations of inns, public conveyances on land or
water, theaters, and other places of amusement."
The disqualification of citizens for jury service "on account of race, color, or previous condition of servitude"
was prohibited. But the Civil Rights Act made no mention of integrating the public schools; that was an issue to
be hammered out by other generations of Americans.
The Civil Rights Act of 1875 was a historical land-
mark. It was the first time the federal government had
directly intervened to end social segregation and
discrimination by states and by private businesses serving the public. *Harper's Weekly* hailed the Act, saying:

It is the completion of the promise of equal civil rights.
. . . Legislation on the subject will not at once remove
all prejudice, but it will clear the way for its disappear-
ance.

The magazine editors had been overly optimistic. Less
than a decade after the passage of the Civil Rights Act, it
was declared unconstitutional by the U. S. Supreme
Court. In 1883, the Court decided that the Fourteenth
Amendment had not given Congress jurisdiction over the
social relationships between Negro and white. It was to
take more than 70 years for the Court to reverse this deci-

sion. In 1954, Chief Justice Earl Warren delivered the unanimous opinion of the Supreme Court that segregation in public education was a denial of the equal protection of the laws. The Court directed that Negroes must be admitted to public schools on a racially nondiscriminatory basis with "all deliberate speed."

XVII

HIGH AMONG the knotty problems that faced the nation after the Civil War was Negro suffrage. At first, no one in the North seemed certain of the path to follow. Even Thaddeus Stevens hedged on the issue. Speaking to his constituents in September 1865, Stevens said:

> Whether those who fought our battles, should all be allowed to vote, or only those of a paler hue, I leave to be discussed in the future when Congress can take legitimate cognizance of it.

This timidity shown by such a fierce Radical stemmed from the political situation in the North, where most states refused to let Negroes vote. Every effort to change this had been defeated. Yankee public opinion definitely ran against giving the ballot to the Negro.

Embarrassed by this condition and fearful of losing public support, the Radicals generally avoided a showdown on the question of suffrage. Even the Fourteenth Amendment skirted the issue. Under the second section

of the Amendment, any state refusing adult male citizens
the right to vote, except for participating in rebellion or
other crimes, was to be punished by having its representation in Congress reduced in proportion to the number
denied the vote. This provision was never implemented,
nor any state penalized, although many violated it by
withholding the vote from Negroes.

The Amendment resulted from compromises between
Radicals and Moderates. At the time of its passage, most
Radicals openly favored Negro suffrage, but they needed
the Moderates to help them hold Congress and frequently made concessions to their more cautious colleagues on controversial issues. Denouncing the voting
provision of the Fourteenth Amendment, Stevens called
it "a shilly-shally bungling thing." To Wendell Phillips it
was a "fatal and total surrender."

Congressman George Julian, discussing the measure,
wrote:

> Of course no man could afford to vote against the
> proposition . . . but it was a wanton betrayal of justice
> and humanity. Congress, however, was unprepared for
> more thorough work. The conservative policy . . . was
> obliged, as usual, to feel its way cautiously and wait on
> the logic of events; while the Negro . . . was finally
> indebted for the franchise to the desperate madness of
> his enemies in rejecting the dishonorable proposition of
> his friends.

Their overwhelming victory at the polls in 1866 em-
boldened Moderate and Radical Republicans to come
out fully for Negro suffrage. A blow in that cause was to

grant voting privileges to Negroes residing in the District of Columbia. The Radical-Moderate-sponsored First Reconstruction Act of 1867 required Southern states to write Negro suffrage into their constitutions.

At last, in 1869, the Fifteenth Amendment was passed and clearly stated: "The right of the citizens of the United States to vote shall not be denied or abridged by the United States or by any State on account of race, color or previous condition of servitude." The Amendment was ratified a year later and a leading publication, *The Nation,* editorialized: "Thus, the agitation against slavery has reached an appropriate and triumphant conclusion."

However, after this first wave of enthusiasm, not only *The Nation,* but also many others, began to worry about the potential aftermath of the Fifteenth Amendment. To their horror, some realized that one day a Negro might be elected to high national office. To favor votes for Negroes had marked one as a high-minded intellectual, a humanitarian. But now that Negro suffrage had become reality, fainthearted liberals became panicky. The prospect of black men in Congress was upsetting enough; but what if a Negro should win even higher office?

Perhaps, only perhaps, it had been a mistake to act so precipitously. After all, the poor Negroes were not quite ready for all the burdens of citizenship; voting was a heavy responsibility. Maybe it had been given to the Negro too soon. Maybe the Negro should have been required to wait patiently a little longer.

Answering this was a proclamation by a group of Negroes in Alabama, which declared:

> There are some good people who are always preaching patience. They would have us wait a few months, years or generations until the whites voluntarily give us our rights, but we do not intend to wait one day longer than we are absolutely compelled to do.

Militant Negroes only frightened genteel liberals. *The Nation* altered its previous position on Negro suffrage. Perhaps it would have been better "to enfranchise the Negro gradually" and through "an educational test." There were suggestions from some quarters that Negro suffrage be postponed until 1876, more than a decade after the war, "when tempers will have cooled and many Negroes will have attained a degree of literacy."

In ringing defense of immediately granting Negroes the vote, Congressman Julian, addressing the House, said:

> A literacy test . . . is a singularly insufficient measure of fitness. Reading and writing are mechanical processes, and a man may perform them without any worthiness of life or character. . . . If penmanship must be made the avenue to the ballot, I fear several honorable gentlemen on this floor will be disenfranchised. . . . More than one half million white men in this country are illiterate, yet no one proposes to take the ballot from them. . . . By no means do I disparage education, and especially political training; but the ballot itself is a schoolmaster. If you expect a man to use it well you must place it in his hands, and let him learn to cast it by trial and

error. . . . If you wish to teach the ignorant man, black or white, how to vote, you must grant him the right to vote as the first step in his education.

When it came to restricting voting privileges for white Southerners, even former Confederate leaders, Congress showed remarkable leniency. The Joint Committee on Reconstruction suggested to Congress that all who had supported the Confederacy should be excluded from voting in federal elections until July 4, 1870. Stevens felt this was not severe enough:

> Here is the mildest of all punishments ever inflicted on traitors. I would be glad to see it extended to 1876, and to include all State and municipal as well as national [elections].

However, the mood of Congress was less stern than that of Stevens. The final version of the penalty to be inflicted on Confederate leaders was a soft one. All who had held state or federal offices before the rebellion, and who had then supported the Confederacy, were to be ineligible for public office until pardoned by a two-thirds congressional vote. This applied to almost the entire political leadership of the prewar South. In 1872, however, Congress passed an amnesty law that allowed all but a few former prominent Confederates to hold public office.

The controversy that boiled around Negro suffrage was part of the broad canvas of Radical Reconstruction. On March 2, 1867, Congress passed the First Reconstruction Act, which outlined in general terms its plan of political Reconstruction. Three subsequent acts (March 23 and July 19, 1867 and March 11, 1868) clarified vague areas of the first one. The later acts provided machinery for carrying out the program and also set up legal means to block any Presidential obstruction to the plan.

As had been anticipated, Johnson vetoed each act when it reached his desk and Congress promptly passed them over his objections. Thus two years after the guns had fallen silent, the complex process of Reconstruction was begun afresh, this time under Radical guidance. They were in control because Johnson's continuing feud with Congress had virtually stripped him of all backing there. Only a few diehard Conservatives and the minority Democrats sided with the President.

The situation in the former Confederate states also helped swing the pendulum to the Radicals. Their behavior was arrogant and unrepentant. Ten of the 11 rebel states dared to reject the Fourteenth Amendment. Terror was rampant throughout the South against Negroes, scalawags and carpetbaggers. Southerners boasted that they were "unreconstructed rebels." These factors turned the Northern public to the Radical view of a harsh peace as mapped by Stevens and his cohorts.

According to the preamble of the First Reconstruction Act, the Radical program was based on the assumption that "no legal governments or adequate protection for life or property . . . exists in the Rebel States." The purpose of the First Act and the three that followed was "the enforcement of peace and good order . . . in said States until loyalty and republican State governments can be legally established."

The first step the Radicals took was to repudiate the Johnson-approved governments and to divide the "unre-constructed" states into five military districts. (The first district was Virginia; the second, North and South Carolina; the third, Georgia; the fourth, Mississippi and Arkansas; the fifth, Louisiana and Texas.) District commanders had full powers "to protect all persons in their rights of person and property, to suppress insurrections, disorder and violence, and to punish . . . all disturbers of the public peace." On their own initiative, District commanders could remove civil officials, arrest and try civilians in military courts, and use federal troops, when necessary, to preserve order.

The responsibility for setting the machinery of the Radical Reconstruction program into motion also fell upon district commanders. They were to supervise the enrollment of all eligible voters including Negroes. When this had been satisfactorily completed, elections for delegates to state constitutional conventions were to be held.

These conventions were obligated to frame a constitution having provisions for Negro suffrage. After the voters had approved the constitution, a governor and a state legislature might be elected. Each legislature had to ratify the Fourteenth Amendment at its first meeting. (After the passage of the Fifteenth Amendment, they had to ratify that, too.) The final step in achieving reconstructed statehood was congressional approval of the newly adopted state constitution; only then was the state entitled to have representation in Washington. While this procedure was running its course, Congress considered the state government to be "provisional only, and in all respects subject to the paramount authority of the United States."

(By 1870, all the rebel states had complied with these Radical conditions and the political Reconstruction of the South was presumed to be complete.)

Reconstruction was only one aspect of the Radical program. As their plan was being implemented in the South, the Radicals were campaigning for the restriction of certain Presidential powers. Radical leaders were worried that Johnson might try to oust them by a military coup. Friends of the President had suggested to him that Congress was sitting illegally because there was no Southern representation in it. A few actually urged Johnson to dissolve Congress by force and to call for new elections. Johnson never would have resorted to such a measure, but the Radicals were taking no chances.

As an initial move to block Johnson, Congress voted itself the right to convene in special session. Prior to the passage of this measure (January 22, 1867), only the President could order such a session. The new law provided that the first session of the Fortieth Congress (elected in 1866) should begin March 4, 1867, instead of early the preceding December as in the past. The Radicals meant to avoid having a long interval between sessions of Congress, a period in which Johnson could pursue his own policies.

In another move to prevent any overt act by the President, Congress restricted his power as the commander in chief of the armed forces. On March 2, 1867, a clause was tacked on to an Army appropriations bill. In this rider the President and the Secretary of War were to issue orders only through the General of the Army, Ulysses S. Grant. The rider stipulated that the headquarters of the General of the Army must remain in Washington; nor was he to be removed or transferred without the consent of the Senate.

The most important legislation by Congress passed on March 2 was the so-called Tenure of Office Act. This provided that a civil officeholder, appointed with consent of the Senate, must continue serving until a successor had been chosen by the President and approved by the Senate.

When the Senate was not in session, the President might remove the man in office and make a temporary replacement. However, should the Senate disapprove of the change at its next session, the former officeholder would "forthwith resume the duties of his office." The Tenure of Office Act referred specifically to members of the Cabinet, who were to hold their posts "during the term of the President by whom they were appointed, and for one month thereafter, subject to the advice and consent of the Senate."

(The purpose of this provision was to keep in office, and prevent the removal by President Johnson, of Edwin M. Stanton, the Secretary of War, the only remaining member of the Cabinet still sympathetic to the Radicals.)

Some Radicals wanted to get Johnson out of the Presidency. These men were convinced that he was a traitor who intended to sabotage the Radical program by putting Southern rebels and Northern copperheads in power. However, the only constitutional way to remove a President from office, unless he voluntarily resigned, was through impeachment for "high crimes or misdemeanors." On strictly legal grounds, Johnson had done nothing to justify impeachment.

Nevertheless, on January 7, 1867, the House approved a resolution by Representative James M. Ashley of Ohio which instructed the Judiciary Committee to "inquire into the conduct of Andrew Johnson . . . and to determine whether or not grounds existed for commencing impeachment proceedings against him." A long and thorough investigation followed. Aided by the Pinkerton National Detective Agency, the Judiciary Committee gathered its evidence against Johnson.

The Judiciary Committee convened on June 3, 1867, to weigh the charges placed against the President. He was accused of illegally returning property to rebels; pardoning men who were still traitors at heart; abusing his veto power; and being implicated in the Lincoln assassination plot. None of these stood up under examination and the Judiciary Committee voted five to four against impeachment.

XVIII

MORE THAN LIKELY, any further efforts at impeachment would have been dropped if not for President Johnson's continued defiance of Congress. No sooner had the Judiciary Committee taken its close vote than he immediately provoked Radical ire and breathed new life into the movement against him.

On January 20, 1867, the President curbed the powers of the five Southern Military District commanders and strengthened the repudiated civil governments. As if this were not enough, Johnson relieved district commanders in sympathy with Radical policies. Congressional tempers, already near the boiling point, spilled over on December 2, 1867, when the President in his annual message stated he "would . . . stand on his rights, and maintain them, regardless of consequences."

Johnson had thrown down the gauntlet to Congress. His defiance brought swift reaction. The Judiciary Committee reversed itself with a five-to-four favoring impeachment. According to the Committee's majority report, Johnson's aim was to reconstruct the Southern states "in accordance with his own will, in the interests of the great criminals who had carried them into rebellion." However, the Committee minority insisted that the President had committed no indictable crime or misdemeanor and added, "There is not a particle of evidence before us which would be received by any court in the land." Apparently this latter opinion carried weight with the House. On December 7, 1867, that body rejected the Judiciary Committee's impeachment recommendation by a vote of 57 to 108.

Once again Johnson had confounded his foes. He seemed to feel that Congress would not dare take a step so drastic as impeaching him and he went on opposing the legislators at every turn. Another showdown came soon enough. In August 1867, while the Senate was not in session, Johnson had dismissed Secretary of War Edwin Stanton from his Cabinet post and replaced him with General Grant, who acepted the position temporarily. Johnson deliberately had violated the Tenure of Office Act because he felt it was unconstitutional and wanted to have a test case of it in Federal Court.

Upon convening, the Senate refused to approve Stanton's removal. Grant then withdrew in favor of his predecessor. Johnson was furious. He accused Grant of "double-crossing" him, claiming that the general had agreed to help him fight the Tenure of Office Act. Grant denied any such arrangement. His feelings ruffled, the general entered into an alliance with the Radicals.

Aided by Grant or not, President Johnson was determined to push his fight against the Tenure of Office Act. On February 21, 1868, he appointed General Lorenzo Thomas as interim Secretary of War and told Stanton to clear out. Backed by the Radicals, Stanton refused to surrender his offices in the War Department building and barricaded himself in them, leaving General Thomas to wander forlornly through the corridors, quite miserable over being a storm center.

Johnson had misjudged Congress and the people of the North. By firing Stanton, who had served so well as Secretary of War, the President not only defied Congress and flouted the Tenure of Office Act, but also angered Northern public opinion. A clamor arose to punish Johnson for his "arrogant" behavior. The public was outraged by this treatment of Stanton.

Congress heeded popular sentiment. On February 24, 1868, the House, in a 126 to 47 vote, resolved that "Andrew Johnson, President of the United States, be impeached of high crimes and misdemeanors in office."

A committee of seven, headed by Thaddeus Stevens, was appointed to draw up the articles of impeachment. By March 2, the Committee had prepared its indictment. It contained 11 articles, the first eight having to do in one way or another with alleged violations of the Tenure of Office Act. The other three charged Johnson with various "high misdemeanors," not the least of which was that he "did attempt to bring into disgrace, ridicule, hatred, contempt and reproach the Congress of the United States."

The trial started March 5 before the Senate with Chief Justice Salmon P. Chase presiding. The impeachment was managed by Congressman Benjamin F. Butler of Massachusetts as the leader of a six-man group. (Thaddeus Stevens, who was to have headed the impeachment team, fell desperately ill and became so enfeebled, that he had to be carried in a chair to and from the impeachment sessions.) Four eminent lawyers, including Henry Stanberry, who had resigned as Attorney General, defended President Johnson.

The impeachment trial dragged on until May 26, 1868. The prosecution needed a two-thirds majority of the Senate to find Johnson guilty. When the vote finally was taken, it tallied 35 for conviction and 19 against, one shy of the required two-thirds majority. Twelve Democrats and seven Republicans had voted to acquit the President.

The critical ballot was cast by Edmond G. Ross of Kansas, a Republican committed to neither the Radicals nor the Conservatives, although frequently siding with the former. Before the impeachment trial, Ross refused to reveal how he would vote. "I shall weigh all the evidence," he said, "and then speak according to the dictates of my conscience."

When the moment came, when the fate of a President hung in the balance, and with the entire nation watching, Ross did not flinch. "I looked down into my open grave," he later wrote, "and then made my decision." It was "Not Guilty." With those words, Ross saved Johnson and wrecked his own career.

He was mercilessly castigated. A Kansas newspaper called him "a poor, pitiful, shriveled wretch." He was accused of accepting a huge bribe for his vote. The New

York *Tribune* described him as "a miserable poltroon and
traitor." Together with the six other Republicans who
had voted for acquittal, Ross was buried under a storm of
abuse. None of the men who stood up for Johnson were
ever again returned to elective office. Only after his
death, some 20 years later, when the passions of the moment had passed, did Ross' detractors recant. "He acted
for his conscience and with a lofty patriotism, regardless
of what he knew must be the ruinous consequences to
himself. He acted right," a Kansas editor said.

Secretary of War Stanton resigned, to be succeeded by
General John M. Schofield, on the heels of the impeachment trial. Despite Radical bitterness at its outcome, the
verdict had been a just one. All charges notwithstanding,
Johnson never plotted treason, nor had he even violated
the Tenure of Office Act. The Act provided that a Cabinet member must serve during the term of the President
who appointed him and for at least one month after.
Since Stanton had been picked by Lincoln, not Johnson,
he was not covered by this clause. The President had
every right to dismiss him. The Radicals, obviously frustrated by Johnson's opposition, had attempted to oust
him for political reasons, not legalistic ones—and they
had failed.

The problem that faced the country was one which
cropped up on several other occasions, before and since,
to bedevil the United States. It was a case of a President
and a Congress at loggerheads. Perhaps the only solution
to such a crisis would be for the President voluntarily to

resign. However, no Chief Executive ever has taken that way out—and probably none ever will.

Johnson completed the remaining months of his term. In November 1868, another Republican, General Ulysses S. Grant, was elected to the Presidency. He took office on March 4, 1869, and Johnson went home to East Tennessee. But he was not quite finished with public life. The Republican Conservatives won full control of his native state in 1874, and the former President returned to Washington as a U.S. Senator.

On March 22, 1875, he delivered his last speech, a scathing attack on Radical Reconstruction. Johnson's oration ended with the words, "God save the Constitution!", an emotional utterance which was his swan song. Shortly after, he was felled by a paralytic stroke and died on July 31, 1875. Symbolically, a copy of the Constitution was placed in his coffin.

XIX

THE TWO ADMINISTRATIONS of General Grant were marked by corruption and rocked by scandals seldom equaled in the country's history. Grant was personally blameless for these ugly incidents except that he placed his trust in men unworthy of it.

Grant also had to cope with the turbulent results of Radical Reconstruction, a stormy era still surrounded by controversy.

During the decade 1867–1877, each state of the former Confederacy fell under Radical control for varying lengths of time. Tennessee, the first state to be captured by the Radicals, was the first to be lost by them—"redeemed," as the white Southern Democrats called their return to power in 1869. The last of the redeemed states were South Carolina, Florida and Louisiana, where the Radicals ruled until 1877.

The Radical Reconstruction period never knew a moment of tranquility. It has been called "The Dark Time," "The Tragic Era," "The Dreadful Decade," "The Age of

Hate." To some, Reconstruction epitomized the shame of the American people—"the depths of national disgrace." It was a time, according to some historians, of unrelieved sordidness, crime and graft, a tyranny under which noble Southerners suffered agonies that scarred future generations. The South was invaded by unscrupulous, grasping carpetbaggers; plundered and looted by crooked politicians; betrayed by degraded scalawags—Southerners who collaborated with the "enemy"; humiliated by ignorant, illiterate, barbarous and sensual Negroes whose aim was to Africanize the South and destroy Caucasian civilization.

As described by anti-Radical critics, the governments inflicted upon the Southern states were run by untrained men, uniformly incompetent, graft-ridden and corrupt. The South's "natural" leaders, experienced statesmen, educated and cultured aristocrats, were removed from the political scene, stripped of power, wealth and position and made to suffer cruelly.

For many years, the Southern version of Radical Reconstruction remained the accepted one, a distorted picture which had the proud South beaten down by Yankee scoundrels and their minions. However, during recent years, certain historians, taking a sharp, unbiased look at the period, have come up with a different interpretation of what happened down South in the 12 years immediately following the Civil War.

An unhappy upper-class Virginian protested in a letter to Thaddeus Stevens that highborn Southerners were being subjected to

our former slaves and the mean white serfs of the earth.
. . . We are the children of the Lees, Clays, Henrys and
Jacksons. . . . Tell me if we are to be ruled by the dregs
of society.

Another Southerner reported that the Radicals in his
native state were "those paying no taxes, riding poor
horses, wearing dirty shirts and having no use for soap."
A Nashville (Tenn.) newspaper called most of "the self-
styled Southern Unionists the merest trash that could be
collected in a civilized community." While the Radicals
were being condemned, the prewar leaders of the South
were hailed as paragons of intellect, breeding, statesman-
ship, integrity and honesty.

Today, revisionists cannot fathom why these antebellum leaders deserved such lavish praise; the men in
charge of the South before and during the Civil War left
much to be desired. Most failed to understand the problems of their times, nor could they find an intelligent solution for them. Their policies had ended in bloodshed,
disaster, and a sacrifice by the Southern masses such as
few peoples ever have been called upon to equal.

Apparently leadership in the Old South did not spring
from ability but rather from economic power and political shrewdness. The landowners, the wealthy, the aristocracy were the men in charge. When ousted by the Radicals, they were missed not for their special endowments,
but for the traditionally accepted presence of their authority. The change in leadership from Conservative to Radical was no great tragedy for the average Southerner. The
deposed politicos had made little contribution to the gen-

eral welfare of the South; the new crop could hardly do worse. Still, the changes aroused the resentments of Southerners. The rich were angry because they had been dethroned; the poor, because the new regimes had been put in power by outsiders.

The carpetbagger was the archvillain of Reconstruction days. He has been presented as a money-hungry, scheming, lustful scoundrel bent on plundering Southern treasure and defiling Southern women. Traditionally, he has been depicted as a Yankee pauper carrying his paltry possessions in a carpetbag and moving from place to place, to feed like a jackal on the wounded South.

This concept of the carpetbaggers was only partially true. There were among them individuals who fitted the accepted description, disreputable men who had rushed South for plunder or political gain. But many were not of that sort.

The original carpetbaggers had come South before 1867, when it was impossible to win political office because the Confederate states were then under martial law. Indeed, carpetbaggers were not all poor men; they were not all ignorant; they were not all corrupt. They were a mixed lot, men and women from every station and walk of life, who had settled in the South for varied reasons that had nothing to do with a desire for personal gain or political power.

Most had migrated because, like the Far West, the South presented a new frontier and fresh opportunity. Some sought to buy cotton lands or to start businesses. Some had come to develop the South industrially, to

build factories, establish insurance companies, open
banks, extend railroads or engage in mercantile, commercial and trading operations.

Some were discharged Union soldiers who had served
below the Mason-Dixon Line during the war and liked
what they found—pleasant climate, good land, a place
for a hardworking, ambitious man to make his mark.

There were those who had come as teachers, field
workers and officials of the Freedmen's Bureau, or as
agents of Northern benevolent societies formed to aid
Negroes. These people were in the South to set up schools
for the ex-slaves, their children, and poor whites. They
distributed food, clothing and medical supplies to all
needy persons. Some bungled their jobs, some worked
well. Some were lazy, crooked or both. Most were honest
and dedicated to their mission.

But the white Southern Conservatives resented every
Yankee settler, especially those who became active in
Radical politics and helped the Negroes. It made no
difference whether the Northerner was honest or dishon-
est; to the Southerner he was a "damned Yankee
carpetbagger," an object of hatred, a target for violence,
a "nigger-loving" troublemaker who had to be taught a
lesson before the South was turned into a "second Africa."

Even more despised by white Southerners were the so-
called scalawags. According to a prominent Alabaman,
scalawags were "cowardly deserters and turncoats, the
lowest element in the South, the depraved, degenerate

trash who had fled the foe in wartime and now came crawling to him with an eye cocked for a soft job."

This definition of the scalawags survived the many decades since the Civil War. However, as in the case of the carpetbaggers, most scalawags were neither cravens, traitors nor sniveling weaklings. The Confederate hero, Lieutenant General James A. Longstreet, one of Lee's ablest corps commanders, was smeared as a scalawag. He moved to New Orleans after the war, became a partner in a cotton brokerage house and headed an insurance firm. By 1867, the general announced that the vanquished must accept the terms of the victors. ("We have fought the good fight and we have lost; now we must clasp the hand of our Northern brothers and march on to rebuild this nation and make it the greatest on earth; Confederates no longer, Unionists no longer, but Americans all, firmly united," declared "Old Pete" Longstreet, as his soldiers once had dubbed him.)

Longstreet joined the Republican party, supported the Radical Reconstruction policy and backed Grant for the Presidency in 1868. From then on, he was rewarded for his work within the Republican party by being given federal jobs. Because of this, "Old Pete" was castigated as a scalawag although he hardly fitted the stereotype: few men had a war record to match his; few had fought so hard for the Confederacy.

There were other leading Confederates who swung over to the Radical cause. James L. Orr of South Carolina, who had been a member of the Confederate Senate, was denounced as a scalawag because he endorsed Radical Reconstruction and accepted a role in carrying out the policy. In a letter, Orr explained why he was willing to face the scorn and abuse of former friends, neighbors and comrades-in-arms, and to accept the label of scalawag. He wrote: "It is important for our prominent men to identify themselves with the Radicals for the purpose of controlling their action and preventing mischief to the state." Thus, while attacked as a scalawag, Orr remained a firm Confederate patriot.

There were thousands such as Longstreet and Orr who accepted the reality of defeat and the terms of the victors. Most Southerners did not want to keep alive the sectional partisanship which had brought on the war. They had had a bellyful of fighting, and yearning for peace, they resolved to attain it at any price.

Also labeled scalawags were Southerners who had been pro-Union during the war and as a result suffered vicious persecution for their beliefs. They not only wanted to see their secessionist neighbors severely punished, but also hoped that, under Radical Reconstruction, political power in the state would fall to them.

Among all Southerners, scalawags and "unreconstructed rebels" alike, there was one common bond: both opposed civil and political rights for Negroes. Scalawags favored disenfranchising their Confederate neighbors so that the state governments would be scalawag-controlled, but they were vehemently against giving Negroes the vote.

The Negroes, because of political inexperience and economic helplessness, were misled and victimized both by Republicans and Southern white Democrats. However, although many former slaves were political puppets, a great number were politically aware and informed. They understood the meaning of suffrage. Winning the right to vote was not something forced by outsiders onto an indifferent mass of Negroes. Negro spokesmen demanded votes not only for the newly freed men, but also for Negroes throughout the United States. When the war had ended, expectations ran high among Negroes that their old dream of winning the vote would be realized. But that long-cherished ambition was denied by the first Johnson governments, which came out with a policy of "votes for whites only."

The freedmen did not accept this supinely. Mass meetings were called all over the South to demand that Congress ensure the vote for Negroes. A meeting of North Carolina freedmen passed a resolution saying:

> We do solemnly resolve that so long as the Federal Government refuses us the right to protect ourselves by means of the ballot . . . we will hold it responsible before God for our protection.

Under Radical Reconstruction, Negroes were allowed to vote in the old Confederate states. Although often disappointed by the Republicans, especially in the matter of "forty acres and a mule," which had been so frequently and glibly promised, the Negroes still rallied to the Republicans and helped win the Presidency for General Grant in 1868.

During the political campaigns of the Reconstruction period, the Democrats tried vainly to woo the Negro vote, but the Democratic commitment to the principle of white supremacy pushed the Negro to the Republicans. Despite this, Southern Democrats clung to their lily-white platform and continued to oppose full political and civil rights for the Negro.

Under the Radicals, the Negroes had enjoyed a taste of American citizenship and even held political office in some Southern states. South Carolina had at different times a Negro lieutenant governor, secretary of state, speaker of the House and an associate justice of the State Supreme Court.

Several officials in Mississippi, Louisiana and Florida were Negroes—all able men of integrity. Even Negro-haters admitted that these officeholders did their jobs well. In additition, 14 Southern Negroes were elected to the U. S. House of Representatives. Two Mississippi Negrocs wcre elected to the U. S. Senate—Hiram R. Revels finished one year of an unexpired term, taking the seat that once had belonged to Jefferson Davis; Blanche K. Bruce won a full Senate term. (Not until 1966 was another Negro, Edward Brooke of Massachusetts, elected to the Senate.)

During Reconstruction, the higher offices of Southern state governments usually were filled by white men. Negroes held some city and county offices but generally were unable to rise beyond state legislatures.

The talents and abilities of Negroes elected or appointed to office varied widely. Some were men of the highest merit, some were incompetents. Just as white politicians, some Negro officeholders were easily corruptible, others unshakably honest.

For better or for worse, the Negro was attaining a place on the American scene; but every step of his ascent was bitterly contested. Whites resented each forward move the Negro made. Their feelings were summed up in the words of a South Carolina planter:

> Radical Reconstruction is unbridled barbarism overwhelming civilization by physical force. . . . It is the slave rioting in the halls of the master and putting the master under his feet.

Radical Reconstruction was nothing of the sort. To be sure, there were many cases of friction between blacks and whites. Sometimes Negroes acted aggressively, but, on the whole, were well-behaved and seldom vindictive. They wanted civil and political rights and little else. Social segregation was not a major issue. One Negro leader in South Carolina speaking on that subject said:

> I venture to say to my white fellow-citizens that we, the colored people, are not in quest of social equality. I for one do not ask to be introduced in your family circle if you are not disposed to receive me there.

Charges were hurled against Radical Reconstruction. There were many accusations of fraud, bribery, corruption and graft, but only a few could be proved. Corruption was rife in some Southern states at different times; but the 1870s was a period of rising graft in high places everywhere. On a national scale, the Crédit Mobilier and the Whiskey Ring were multimillion-dollar scandals which involved members of Congress and others in high government circles close to President Grant. There were unsavory Republican administrations in several Northern states. But corruption crossed party lines during the Gilded Age of the 1870s. The worst band of grafters ever to hold political sway in any metropolis fleeced New York City of many millions of dollars. This was the so-called Tweed Ring, made up of Tammany Hall Democrats. Their staggering thievery amounted to more than the corruption in all the Southern states put together.

Despite all the shortcomings, failures and mistakes of Radical Reconstruction, the state governments which ruled in that period possibly were the most liberal and democratic the South ever had known. No matter how bitterly white Conservatives assailed the Radicals, the truth could not be hidden. For the first time in Southern history, Negroes were granted full civil and political equality, and the state governments were pledged to protect them in the enjoyment of these rights.

But Radical Reconstruction lasted only a few short years. Too soon, the old order replaced the new. The white Conservatives who "redeemed" their states by ousting the Radicals did no service for democracy. In the so-called redeemed states, Negroes and poor whites were once again relegated to political and economic obscurity.

Their brief moment of some equality ran out. Not until the middle of the twentieth century were Negroes to regain the few rights they had won—and lost—in the era of Radical Reconstruction.

XX

GENERAL ULYSSES S. GRANT had proven himself to be a top-notch field commander, a courageous soldier, a generous victor. He was a man who could handle regiments, divisions, corps and armies, but lacked the acumen, talent and skill to be President of the United States.

In the corruption- and scandal-torn eight years of his two administrations, the Radical grip on the South was broken. By 1876, the Democrats had recaptured eight Southern states: Tennessee in 1869; Virginia and North Carolina, 1870; Georgia, 1871; Alabama, Arkansas and Texas, 1874; and Mississippi, 1875. Only three states—Flordia, Louisiana and South Carolina—still remained in Radical hands in 1876.

After the presidential election that year, a neck-and-neck race won by the Republican candidate, Rutherford B. Hayes, the Democrats reclaimed the last three Confederate states. Hayes accepted this loss and withdrew the last federal forces from the South in April 1877. Florida, Louisiana and South Carolina rejoined the fold. According to white Conservatives, the South was "redeemed"; Reconstruction, the so-called Tragic Era, was over.

Now that the federal government had renounced all responsibility for the Reconstruction program, the Negroes were abandoned to the not-so-tender mercies of the Southern white power bloc. All that Radical leaders had feared would happen, should the U.S. government pull out of the South, came to pass. The rebels were triumphant. The old masters of the South once again held the reins and cracked the whip.

The only apparently durable aspect of Northern victory was the continuing presence of the 11 Confederate states within the framework of the Union. The desperate stab at secession had failed and never would be tried again, although some Southern states maintained a truculent attitude toward the Union. The shibboleth of states' rights was to be raised many times during the years ahead.

The only other lasting result of the war was the adoption of the Thirteenth, Fourteenth and Fifteenth Amendments to the Constitution. Slavery no longer existed, according to the law of the land. But whether the Negro's lot as a freedman under the Conservatives would be more desirable than slavery was a moot point. The redeemed South obeyed the Thirteenth Amendment—slavery no longer was practiced—but the Fourteenth and Fifteenth Amendments, intended to make meaningful the Negro's freedom, were openly flouted in the South. The states once again set the standards for voter qualifi-

cations; in most cases Negroes were excluded because of
property requirements, literacy tests, poll taxes and any
number of local ordinances aimed at keeping the blacks
from the polls.

Before long the Negro was once again standing hum-
bly and servilely in the presence of whites. It was a deg-
radation much harder to accept than that of the past. The
Negro had known a touch of equality; he had learned
how joyous freedom might be.

By the time this came about, most of the old Radical
firebrands had burned out—some had died, some no
longer held office, some simply had lost their zeal for the
crusade. In August 1868, Thaddeus Stevens succumbed
to the illness which had been tormenting him for years.
The news of his death brought rejoicing in every corner
of the South. One Southern editor exulted, "The prayers
of the righteous have at last removed the Congressional
curse!"

In one way or another, the Radical ranks were de-
pleted; all the steam seemed to be going out of the great
movement for social reform that had gained such
strength in the early post–Civil War years. The Republican party no longer cared to carry on the fight for the
Negro in the South, to render him economic aid, to provide him with educational opportunities. The task of
Radical Reconstruction seemed at an end; the tide was
shifting.

At one time there had been fervent sentiment to keep
the South under Washington's thumb. But that feeling
was rapidly becoming dispelled. There was much disen-

chantment with the course of Radical Reconstruction; also the progress made by the Negro as a freedman proved disappointing to many well-meaning, but impatient Republicans.

Also, the people were tired of having the "bloody shirt" waved at them. The bulk of Northern people wanted to forget the war after five, six, ten years. As far as they were concerned, the South had been punished; after all, in the words of a former Radical:

> We could not go on forever on memories of the past. . . . We needed not the fostering of sectional hate but oblivion of the past, and an earnest . . . endeavor to grapple with questions of practical administration.

The once staunch Radical, George W. Julian, writing his memoires in 1884, stated: "By the 1870's, many regarded the Republican Party as a spent political force . . . which threatened to outlast its mission." In listing the new problems that faced the nation, Julian stressed corruption, reform of the Civil Service, tariff and monetary issues as the burning questions of the day; significantly, he failed even to mention the plight of the Southern Negroes.

The floundering Republican party was torn by factionalism. In the past there had been the Moderate-Radical bloc against the Conservatives, but the Radical wing dominated the party. In Grant's first term, many Republicans broke with the President; they differed on numerous questions, not the least of which was the matter of continuing to fight for Negro civil and political rights.

Those who felt that a Southern Republican party could be maintained by Negro votes, remained loyal to Grant and carried on the fight for the Negro. This group, calling themselves Stalwarts, were hard-boiled, practical politicians; they had no great sympathy for the Negroes, but saw in them a potent power which they intended to control.

Unlike the Radicals, the Stalwarts expected no tremendous changes in the Negro, no miraculous transformation from illiterate slave to alert citizen. The liberal do-gooders abandoned the Negro because he did not come up to the standards they had set for him; and, at the same time, the reformers condemned the Stalwarts for "playing politics" with the Negro.

As the Republicans were losing strength and becoming too involved in intraparty squabbles, the Southern Democrats grew stronger. This was largely because of the general amnesty passed by Congress in May 1872. The act restored full rights to most former Confederates who were barred from holding office by the Fourteenth Amendment. This restored to active politics thousands of old-line rebel leaders, men who had enjoyed much influence in antebellum days, and still retained their former hold on the community. With such men now available as candidates, the white men of the South rallied to their support and returned them to various offices with overwhelming majorities.

But it was not only the weakening of the Republican party on a national scale, or the reappearance of the old

Southern leaders, that undermined Radical Reconstruction. Racial prejudice was a cancer in the body of the country. Like that deadly disease, prejudice and hatred spread through the system, destroying all it touched. This existed in the North as well as the South. Only a minority of Yankees ever had felt any real enthusiasm for the Radical attempt to obtain civil and political equality for the Negro.

Because the Negro had not bounded forward and improved his station with remarkable alacrity, the false assumption spread that he was inferior to the white. The fainthearted reformers, so quick to downgrade the Negro, never seemed to consider that many thousands of whites—North and South—lived in ignorance, poverty and economic backwardness; nor had the benevolent aid of charity workers lifted them from the depths. The myopic men who turned from the Negro failed to see that environment, not race, maimed and stunted, destroyed initiative, warped minds and crippled potential. The industrial white slave of the North, chained to a factory machine, browbeaten and crushed by poverty, barely able to exist on his meager salary, was as deprived as the black ex-slave who did not yet know how to use his freedom.

"I am convinced," declared a well-known minister after a trip through the South, "that the Negro as he is, no matter how educated, is not the mental equal of the Caucasian."

Such a generalization was lapped up by Negro-baiters;

but it was mild compared to the ravings of Northern Democrats who stirred race hatred to turn Yankee support from the Radical Reconstruction program. Senator Thomas Hendricks of Indiana, the Democratic minority leader, once told a crowd of white workingmen:

> I say that . . . this is a white man's government, made by the white man for the white man. . . . I'm against giving the colored man a vote, because I think we should remain a political community of white people. . . . I'm against mixing the races. I want to see the white race kept a white race! And I don't want to see our shops and factories flooded with cheap black labor. . . . In plain language . . . I don't want to see the black take away the white man's bread!

Such chauvinistic oratory had its effect; workers, fearing that the Republicans would bring up hordes of Negroes from the South as a source of cheap labor, cast their votes for the Democrats.

Other voices aided the anti-Negro litany. In 1870, Nathaniel S. Shaler, a Southerner who had fought with the Union Army, wrote an article for the *Atlantic Monthly*, a magazine widely read by Northern intellectuals. Shaler's piece professed to give informed observations on the Negro. Among Shaler's comments was one on education of Negroes:

> The School . . . has its place in civilization, but it is the last step in the development of a race, not the first, and its value consists in the fact that it is the final result of the education of a thousand years of effort; and when we undertake to civilize a race as foreign to us in every trait as the Negroes, by imposing on them this final

product of our national growth, we wrong ourselves and them.

Which was a fairly highflown way of saying that the Negro should not be educated, but preferably kept in a state of blissful ignorance.

XXI

WHILE ANTI-NEGRO RACISTS were having a field day in the North, the average Southerner kept up his undeclared war against the Radical governments. No matter how beneficial these state administrations might have been, the very fact that they were committed to equal civil rights for both races and were supported by Negro votes, fanned opposition to them among poor white farmers, mechanics and laborers.

These low-income, low-status whites hated and feared the Negro; for they were well aware that free Negroes, given the opportunity, would offer competition for jobs, land and even social position.

Downtrodden themselves, the poor whites had to browbeat someone—and the Negro was the best available victim. They backed the Democrats because that party told them it was against the black and for the white race. It was the "white man's party." The lower-class white man believed the Negro was his inferior because he wanted to believe it; in a life of struggle there was precious little he had to brag about except the color of his skin. White was better than black and that was that. "I am a white man," he brayed. "A white man! I'm going to make the niggers respect me because I'm white and they ain't!"

The richer, upper-strata Southerner also preached white supremacy—not because he feared competition from the Negro, but because he wanted to keep the ex-slaves as a cheap labor source. It mattered little to the landed Southerner, the merchant, banker, manufacturer or insurance executive whether Negroes could or could not vote. "We'll control them one way or the other," a wealthy merchant said. "We'll persuade him to support us; it won't be hard to find a Negro leader or two who'll sing our song."

In 1876, the great Confederate cavalryman, Wade Hampton, running for governor of South Carolina on the Democratic ticket, told a Negro meeting:

> I want your votes; I don't want you to be deprived of them. . . . I pledge my faith, and I pledge it for those gentlemen who are on the ticket with me, that if we are elected, as far as in us lies, we will observe, protect and defend the rights of the colored man as quickly as any man in South Carolina.

This was strange talk coming from an aristocratic former slaveowner—but it was good politics. No one, black or white, would ever disbelieve the word of a gentleman such as Wade Hampton. What Southerner—black or white—would trust an alien carpetbagger before he did Wade Hampton? The answer was, very few. Hampton promised the Negroes his protection and no man doubted him. He was a Southern cavalier, a gallant soldier, a man of honor.

And Wade Hampton also was a clever politician. He had long since accepted the inevitability of Negro suffrage and knew what to do about it:

> We must direct the Negro vote . . . Now how shall we go about this? Simply by making the Negro a Southern man, and if you will, a Democrat, anything but a Radical.

For Wade Hampton, politics had no color line. A vote was a vote, whether from a black man or a white one.

However, all Southern politicians were not Wade Hamptons. It was far simpler for them to garner votes by calling on race prejudice and bigotry when appealing to lower-class whites. In the North, the Radicals waved the "bloody shirt"; in the South, "white supremacy" was the equivalent of that tactic.

Democratic newspapers and speakers spewed hatred of Negroes. In the lexicon of bigotry, the Negro male constantly menaced the purity of Southern womanhood. Racists warned that the ultimate aim of the Radicals was to populate the South with a "mongrel" race which would "Africanize" their beloved Dixie. They raised the slogan, "A white man in a white man's place! A black man in a black man's place!"

This was crude propaganda, but effective. In state after state, as the opportunity arose, Radical candidates were defeated at the polls, sometimes peacefully, sometimes violently.

Organized violence and terrorism against scalawags, carpetbaggers, Radicals and Negroes were rampant in the South. The rope, bullet and torch cut a swath across the Confederacy as Southerners fought what they called "an unjust and tyrannical power." Vicious and brutal acts were justified as "self defense" by those who perpetrated them against "the scoundrels who have filled our land with mourning, beggared us, freed our slaves and as a last insult and injury, made the ex-slave a political equal. . . . What red-blooded man can endure such infamy?" a Southerner asked a Northern newspaperman.

Groups were formed to inflict a reign of brutality against the "enemies of the South." The best known of these gangs was the Ku Klux Klan, founded in 1866 at Pulaski, Tennessee, by some young Confederate officers. Started as a fraternity of sorts, the Klan quickly became an instrument aimed at keeping Negroes "in their place" and "stamping out the human vermin infesting the South." Other terror bands were the Knights of the White Camelia, the White Brotherhood, the Pale Faces and the '76 Association.

None reached the membership or the power of the Klan. Poor whites, "mudsills," lower-class workers, toughs and hoodlums flocked to join the Klan, attracted by the elaborate ritualistic trappings, the robe and hood uniform and the chance to unleash naked force against "uppity niggers" and "meddling Yankee carpetbaggers."

The Klan was organized in small local units called Dens. The Dens were organized into Provinces; the Provinces, into Dominions; the Dominions into Realms; and the whole into an empire—"The Invisible Empire of the South." At the head was the Grand Wizard and ten Genii; then came the Grand Dragons, the Furies, the Hydras, the Nighthawks. Den members were called Ghouls and the Den Master was entitled the Cyclops.

All this mythological mumbo jumbo was enhanced by blood vows and weird initiation ceremonies. The Klan creed, a high-sounding declaration, stated:

> This is an institution of Chivalry, Humanity, Mercy and Patriotism . . . embodying in its genius and its principles all that is chivalric in conduct, noble in sentiment, generous in manhood and patriotic in purpose.

The Klan's goal was "to protect the weak, the innocent and the defenseless. . . . To protect and defend the Constitution of the United States." These worthy aims were to be pursued by men who pledged themselves as "opposed to Negro equality, both social and political" and "in favor of a white man's government."

Dressed in white robes and hoods, riding white-sheeted horses, the Klansmen galloped through the night spreading fear amongst Radicals both Negro and white. They raided Radical meetings, horsewhipped carpetbaggers and scalawags, murdered Negroes, killed, burned and plundered, in marked contrast to their lofty ideals of "Chivalry, Humanity, Mercy and Patriotism."

These acts of lawlessness grew so out of hand that some Klan leaders tried to disband the organization; but they had unleased evil forces which they no longer could control. The Klan was eventually stopped, but Congress had to do it. After investigating the explosive situation, Congress passed two so-called Force Acts, the first on May 31, 1870 and on the second on February 28, 1871. These ordinances provided that the use of force or intimidation to prevent citizens from voting was to be punished by fine or imprisonment. They authorized the President to use the military to enforce the Fifteenth Amendment.

On April 20, 1871, the Ku Klux Klan Act was passed. This imposed heavier penalties on persons who

> shall conspire together, or go in disguise . . . for the purpose . . . of depriving any person or any class of persons of the equal protection of the laws . . . or of equal privilege . . . under the laws.

Federal troops were reinforced in the South and President Grant suspended the writ of habeas corpus in those areas where the Klans were most active. After dozens of arrests, fines and imprisonments, the Klan was finally suppressed. By 1872 it had almost disappeared. (During the 1950s and 1960s, with renewed agitation for Negro rights, the hooded terror organization reappeared. It had previously enjoyed a brief rebirth in certain parts of the country in the 1920s.)

The fall of the Klan did not end violence in the South. Mississippi became a hotbed of terror. The Democrats

there used what was known as the "Mississippi Plan." A
newspaper baldly described the Mississippi Plan in these
terms:

> All other means having been exhausted to abate the
> horrible condition of things, the thieves and robbers, and
> scoundrels, white and black, deserve death and ought to
> be killed. . . . We shall carry the election peaceably if
> we can, forcibly if we must.

To implement the Plan, local Democrats formed rifle
clubs. They drilled, held target practice, and paraded
through Negro neighborhoods as a warning. They broke
up Republican meetings at gunpoint and provoked riots
in which hundreds of Negroes were killed. Armed men
patrolled roads leading to registration places and polling
booths. Any Negro caught heading in that direction was
certain to get shot or beaten. These tactics so terrified
Negroes that they were afraid to register or to vote.

In September 1875, with a statewide election sched-
uled for November, Adelbert Ames, the Radical governor
of Mississippi, ordered all rifle clubs disbanded. His proclamation was mocked by Democrats, who responded, "If
you want us dispersed, come on and try to do it!"

Ames sought to recruit state militia to keep law and
order, but the only volunteers were Negroes; the Governor knew that arming them would set off a vicious race
war. He appealed to Washington for help, but received
double-talk instead of troops. When election day rolled
around, Ames could only pray that there would be no
general massacre of colored people in Mississippi.

Cowed Negroes stayed away from the polls in droves.

Thousands hid in the swamps. No Negro dared approach a polling place unless accompanied by whites who were known Democrats and could give assurances that the black man was going to vote for that party. In some localities, Negroes came to the polls in groups, but were shot at, severely beaten and driven off. Small wonder that the Democrats easily won that election and Mississippi entered the ranks of the "redeemed" states.

Noting the success achieved under the Mississippi Plan, Democrats in Florida, Louisiana and South Carolina followed suit in 1876 and overthrew their Radical governments. The days of Radical Reconstruction were over and the South rejoiced.

The victory of the Conservatives was not accomplished through intimidation and violence alone. These methods could have been countered by the Grant administration; stern military action could have crushed the terrorists. The government in Washington failed to enforce the Fourteenth and Fifteenth Amendments, the Force Acts, and the Civil Rights Acts. Instead of taking resolute measures, the Republicans supinely yielded and let the Democrats take over by default.

There were many reasons for this Federal reluctance to smash the white terror in the South. The Republican alliance with the Negroes had been an uneasy one from the start. Southern Negroes joined the Republican party to get land, to win civil and political rights and because Southern white Democrats treated them hostilely. The Negroes were given no land and the Republican party, under Grant, became more concerned with furthering

Northern business interests than the welfare of the
Negro. By 1876, the Negroes had perceptibly cooled toward the Republicans.

Besides, the Negroes were growing too militant for the
tastes of Yankee industrialists. Here and there, Negro
workers were organizing; in some places they even went
on strike for higher wages and better working conditions.
"If this continues," a Northern Republican politician said
in 1870, "the blacks will become as dangerous to the social order as Anarchists or Communists. . . . We want
no black revolutionaries here!"

Also, Northern financiers were unhappy about the turbulence in the South; such unrest was bad for business.
They urged the Grant Republicans to make a deal with
white Southern Democrats. A way had to be found to
smooth things over. The Southerners stated their terms
bluntly: "Get rid of the Radicals! We'll take care of the
blacks!" A leading New York capitalist, William E.
Dodge, agreed with the Southerners; in a speech to a
business club, he said:

> What the South now needs is capital to develop her
> resources, but this she cannot obtain until confidence in
> her state governments can be restored, and this will
> never be done by federal bayonets. . . . As merchants
> we want to see the South gain her normal condition in
> the commerce of the country. . . . As for the Southern
> Negro . . . it was a mistake to make them feel that the
> United States government was their special friend,
> rather than those with whom their lot is cast, among

whom they must live, and for whom they must work. . . . We have tried this long enough. Now let the South alone.

These were the sentiments of Yankee Big Business. By this time, many Southern Conservatives had been won over to the idea of a "New South" in which commerce and industry would be emphasized. They now could be relied upon to welcome warmly Northern investors. Thus, to the money men, Reconstruction had become more nuisance than necessity.

In 1873 a financial panic shook the nation. So did the exposure of ugly scandals in the Grant administration. Grant, the military hero, while personally not involved in the terrible corruption that blackened his second term, was associated in the public mind with the unsavory dealings of his colleagues.

The financier Jay Cooke, for many years regarded as a paragon of honesty, went bankrupt because of reckless splurging in railroad securities. Even that model of comportment, the renowned Reverend Henry Ward Beecher, had become entangled in a messy personal scandal which ended in a sensational trial for adultery. To many middle-class Americans, these events were signs of national moral decay; the country was indeed in a sorry state if such men as Beecher, Grant and Cooke could no longer be counted upon to uphold standards.

The liberal magazine, *The Nation,* had a remedy. The time had come to give the South home rule. Only then would the country

once more resume the path of careful and orderly progress from which the slavery agitation and its consequences have during the last generation driven us.
. . . It were better that all the blacks and whites now
living south of the Mason and Dixon line were sunk in
the sea than go on as we are going.

Disturbed about the business collapse, unemployment,
falling farm prices and the decline of public and private
morals, Northerners grew sick of Reconstruction and
temporarily lost faith in the Republican party. They no
longer cared about Reconstruction, the emotion of the
war and the "bloody shirt." The voters proved it in 1874,
when the Republicans lost control of the House of Representatives for the first time since before the Civil War.

With Democrats in control, all chance was lost for
federal protection of the Negroes. By 1876, Congress refused to vote funds to keep troops in the South. The
North was frankly bored by the tales of "Southern out-
rages by Negroes."

"We fought the war to end slavery—not to take care
of the blacks forever," a New York newspaper cynically
stated.

When the Mississippi Plan was employed, the federal
government refused to do anything about it. An Ohio
politician warned Grant that, if he sent troops to Mississippi, the Republicans "had less chance than a snowball
in hell to hold Ohio."

The 1874 presidential election campaign between Republican Rutherford B. Hayes and Democrat Samuel Til-
den ended in an electoral-college dispute. To secure the

peaceful inauguration of Hayes, the Republicans had to make concessions to Southern Democrats. If the Democrats supported Hayes and let him take office without incident, the Republicans promised to withdraw all troops from the South and to call off the Reconstruction program. The Southerners agreed. In April 1877, Hayes kept his word. The last Federal forces marched out of Dixie.

An era had ended. All the idealism and the sacrifice of the 12 years that followed the end of the Civil War went down the drain. Southern society remained virtually unchanged; slavery was abolished, but sharecropping took its place and the mass of Negroes remained as propertyless and dependent as serfs.

In the years following the Reconstruction period, despite the Fourteenth and Fifteenth Amendments, the Negro was increasingly denied political and civil rights, and still was the victim of segregation, still a social outcaste. In 1883, the Supreme Court invalidated the Civil Rights Act of 1875; in 1896, the Court came out with the "separate but equal" theory, which sanctioned social segregation. Slaves no more, but second-class citizens still, Negroes were all but forgotten by the Republican party.

However, the Fourteenth and Fifteenth Amendments kept alive the vision of a better day. Decades later, that day began dawning when the Civil Rights struggles of the 1950s and 1960s fanned into flame the smoldering embers of Negro hopes.

Bibliography

In writing this book I consulted many sources and reference works. Those readers who wish to delve more deeply into the Reconstruction period will find *The Era of Reconstruction: 1865–1877* by Kenneth M. Stampp (New York, 1965) an excellent overall study of that era from a revisionist viewpoint. Claude G. Bowers, *The Tragic Era* (Boston, 1929) presents the Reconstruction from the traditional interpretation, as does James G. Randall in *The Civil War and Reconstruction* (Boston, 1937). The classic traditional presentation of Reconstruction is *Reconstruction, Political And Economic, 1865–1877* by William A. Dunning (New York, 1907). *The Angry Scar* by Hodding Carter (New York, 1959) also shows the era in the same light.

A splendid survey of the Reconstruction years is found in *Reconstruction After the Civil War* by John Hope Franklin, a Negro. Another Negro historian, William E. DuBois, presents a fine picture of the Negro's struggle for equality during the period in *Black Reconstruction* (New York, 1935). *The Negro in the Civil War* by Herbert Aptheker (New York, 1938) offers a good discussion of the Negro role in the war, despite the author's obvious Marxist bias.

The best work on Lincoln and Reconstruction is *Lincoln*

the President (4 vols., New York, 1945–1955) by James Randall (Volume IV, *The Last Full Measure* was written with Richard Current.)

James M. McPherson in *The Struggle for Equality: Abolitionists and Negroes in the Civil War and Reconstruction* (Princeton, 1964) gives an incisive analysis of the role played by abolitionists during the Reconstruction period. Two books in defense of the Radicals are *Thaddeus Stevens: A Being Darkly Wise and Rudely Great* by Ralph Korngold (New York, 1955) and *Stanton: The Life and Times of Lincoln's Secretary of War* by Benjamin P. Thomas and Harold M. Hyman (New York, 1962).

There are many more books which delve into the Reconstruction story. Those mentioned above are merely a sampling of the literature on the subject.

I found invaluable in helping me understand the period the contemporary newspapers and magazines available for study. Readers with access to libraries that have these collections would benefit from looking through newspapers such as *The New York Tribune* and magazines such as *The Nation* for the years of the Reconstruction period.

Index

THIS BOOK WAS SET IN

CALEDONIA AND CASLON ANTIQUE TYPES,

PRINTED AND BOUND BY

H. WOLFF BOOK MANUFACTURING COMPANY, INC.

TYPOGRAPHY AND DESIGN ARE BY

LARRY KAMP